THE NORTH AMERICAN
MUSTANG

M J Hardy

David & Charles Aircraft Family Monographs
The Lockheed Constellation by M. J. Hardy
The Focke Wulf Fw 190 by G. Swanborough
and W. Green
The de Havilland Mosquito by M. J. Hardy

THE NORTH AMERICAN
MUSTANG

M J Hardy

"LITTLE ONE"

David & Charles
Newton Abbot London

Title page illustration:—

A day at the races—Lyle Shelton's ground crew
sit it out under his P–51D Mustang N66111
'Little One' at the 1965 National Championships
at Reno (*HL*)

British Library Cataloguing in Publication Data
Hardy, Michael John
  The North American Mustang. – (David and
  Charles aircraft family monographs).
  1. Mustang (Fighter planes)
  I. Title
  623.74'64   TL686.N6

  ISBN 0–7153–7624–1

Typeset by Trade Linotype Ltd., Birmingham
and printed in Great Britain
by Redwood Burn Ltd., Trowbridge
for David & Charles (Publishers) Limited
Brunel House   Newton Abbot   Devon

Contents

Introduction

Quite by chance the first three military types in the David & Charles Aircraft Family Monographs series—the de Havilland Mosquito, the Focke-Wulf Fw 190 and the North American Mustang, the subject of this volume—all had one thing in common, apart from being among the most outstanding combat aircraft of World War II. All three were the product of firms which had not previously attempted the design of an advanced high-performance combat aircraft, and were much more familiar with the lower end of the speed scale, in particular the design of trainers and light transports. This lack of experience of high-speed aircraft might have seemed a serious handicap to any hopes of producing a world-beater; on the contrary, it enabled the de Havilland, Focke-Wulf and North American teams to set entirely new standards of excellence with the Mosquito, Fw 190 and Mustang because of the freshness of approach they brought to the design thinking behind these aircraft. The success of all three served to overturn some long-cherished beliefs: the Mosquito dispelled the notion that an unarmed bomber could

not be made fast enough to outpace defending fighters; the Fw 190 showed that a radial-engined fighter could be the equal of any of its contemporaries with a cleaner liquid-cooled in-line engine; and the Mustang, by means of its laminar flow wing, demonstrated that effective fighter escort could be provided for bombers over ranges that would have been thought impossible before the war.

The Mustang's combination of speed, range and manoeuvrability made it undoubtedly the best of all the wartime American fighters, and in 1943 the Truman Senate War Investigating Committee rated it as 'the most aerodynamically perfect pursuit plane in existence'. High praise indeed—but the Mustang owed its existence to a British specification and orders, not to any US Army Air Force requirement; Britain placed the first orders that enabled North American to gear itself up for large-

P–51D–10–NA Mustang 44–14507: C5–E 'Tangerine' of the 364th Fighter Sqn, 357th Fighter Group, US 8th Air Force, flown by Capt Richard A. Peterson, landing at Liston, Suffolk, October 1944 (*USO*)

scale production of the type, while USAAF interest in the Mustang, which was eventually to re-equip all but one of the Eighth Air Force P-47 Thunderbolt groups in Britain, was surprisingly slow to awaken. This was admitted after the war by General 'Hap' Arnold, when he said that it had been the USAAF's own fault that the Mustang had not been employed operationally very much earlier. Not only that, but this excellent fighter only really began to fulfil its potential when fitted with a British engine, the Packard-built Rolls-Royce Merlin 61 series with two-stage, two-speed superchargers to overcome the lack of performance at height of the Allison V-1710 engine of initial production versions. British initiative and the advice of experts such as Air Marshal Sir Trafford Leigh-Mallory played no small part in this decision, and Rolls-Royce converted the first five Mustangs to Merlin power at its Flight Development Establishment at Hucknall in 1942, as a result of which large-scale production of Merlin-powered versions was initiated in the States.

Britain's part in the Mustang success story is worth emphasising not only as a matter of historical interest but because it contains an important lesson for today,

Ken Burnstine's racing P-51D Mustang N69QF with red and yellow checkerboard tail and wing tips at Mojave, 1975 (HL)

namely the need for national self-confidence in aviation policy making and procurement. Too often in recent years, because major British aircraft projects have been cancelled and the United Kingdom has had to buy from America to fill the resulting needs, and all too often because the quality of British political management has been frankly unequal to the demands of creating a sensible aviation policy, the British have fallen into a kind of psychological dependence on the United States, believing that Britain cannot hope to match that country's technical and design skills, and that the best hope may well be in becoming a kind of glorified subcontractor to US aerospace, as Britain can no longer afford to go it alone with any major new designs. The Mustang's success story as an Anglo-American project owes a great deal to British influence, and shows what a vital part one partner can play in an international collaborative venture even though the end product may bear an American or foreign name, and here the Mustang unwittingly set a pattern for today's collaborative ventures such as Concorde and the A-300B Airbus.

After the war the Mustang saw service in Korea and was used in the little-known 'Football War' of 1969 between El Salvador and Honduras, so called because it arose out of a World Cup elimination match between the two countries. New counter-insurgency versions of the type with Rolls-Royce Dart and Lycoming T55 turboprops appeared, but it was to meet the demands of air racing that some of the most technically interesting variants were produced. Wing tip radiators, wing leading edge radiators, cropped wings, the so-called 'wet wing', heavily boosted engines and oversize props have all been used in the quest by racing pilots to eliminate drag and to squeeze those last few miles per hour from their aircraft. One of the most interesting of these racing versions is one re-engined with a Rolls-Royce Griffon 57 driving a six-blade contra-rotating airscrew. It is nearly forty years now since the Mustang first flew, yet still the process of modifying it for racing goes on—tribute indeed to the versatility and soundness of the basic design.

M. J. HARDY
Selsey, Sussex

Howard Keefe's racing P–51D Mustang N991R
'Miss America' at Mojave, 1975, in its attractive
red, white and blue colour scheme (*HL*)

1 Birth of a Thoroughbred

It is not a little ironical, in view of the dominant position of the US aerospace industry in today's world markets, to recall the extent to which that dominance is based on the foundation stones of large British and French orders for military aircraft placed in the States between April 1938 and Pearl Harbour. When the first British air mission in the States began to visit the US aircraft industry in the spring of 1938 they found it in a state of depression worse than that of the British industry before Britain's rearmament programme began to get under way. The US firms responded with alacrity to the prospects of the big British and French orders being dangled before them; in only forty-eight hours Lockheed produced from scratch a full-size mock-up of a reconnaissance bomber version of their Model 14 airliner, and 200 were promptly ordered as the Hudson for Coastal Command. The other big order placed in 1938 by the British mission was one with North American Aviation Inc for 200 NA–16 advanced trainers, which became the Harvard I in RAF service, and this order was later doubled; ultimately over 5,000 Harvards of all marks were supplied to the British Commonwealth air forces alone, including a few built to French contracts that were taken over by Britain after the fall of France in 1940.

When war broke out President Roosevelt had had to enforce an arms embargo, but on 4 November 1939 Congress passed the 'Cash and Carry' Act permitting Britain and France to purchase aircraft and other arms for cash and take them away in their own ships. Not long after, a joint Anglo-French Purchasing Board was set up and this proceeded to flood the US industry with orders with the intention not just of getting specific aircraft and other items of equipment supplied, but of gearing up American industry to large-scale production to fulfil the role later to be described by President Roosevelt as 'the arsenal of democracy'. British money was spent, not only on the actual hardware but also, in some cases, on building entire factories in the States. By December 1940, two months after the

Mustang prototype had first flown, Britain had ordered the staggering total of 11,000 aircraft (including French contracts taken over after that country's collapse) and had received permission from the American Priorities Board to order another 12,000 aircraft. On paper, this was very impressive although the actual deliveries, in the nature of things, took time to build up: only 104 aircraft were shipped to Britain in the first half of 1940 and 557 went to France in the same period. But when, after Pearl Harbour, America's own military requirements increased sharply, it was the British and French orders that provided the cornerstone for the expansion of US production, and it is reckoned that the beginning of this was made possible some three years earlier than would have been feasible through American orders alone. The history of the war would have been very different had this gearing up of American production not taken place, and the global conflict would certainly have gone on much longer.

It was against this background of frenetic military buying by Britain and France that the Mustang had its genesis. Up to 1941 North American was best known for its NA–16 family of two-seat trainers; the NA–16 prototype, with open cockpits and a fixed undercarriage, had flown in April 1935. The first offshoot of this line was the BT–9 basic trainer with enclosed cockpits for the US Army Air Corps, of which nearly 1,000 were built by North American, and more by other countries under licence; the Royal Canadian Air Force used a similar version and named it Yale. Several armed versions of the basic BT–9 were exported to Latin American and other air forces before the war. This line was followed by the AT–6 family, known as the Harvard to the RAF and the Texan to the USAAF; US Navy variants were designated SNJ–1 to SNJ–6. The AT–6 series evolved from the fixed undercarriage BC–1 basic combat trainer of 1938, and over 15,000 were built by North American during 1938–45. The Harvard/Texan was by far the most widely used Allied trainer of the war, and in it thousands of pilots were taught in Canada and Rhodesia under the Commonwealth Air

Training Plan. It was also built under licence abroad, 755 in Australia by Commonwealth Aircraft Corp as the Wirraway, 2,610 by Noorduyn in Canada, 136 by Saab in Sweden and a total of 176 in Japan. From 1951 to 1954 Cancar in Canada built 555 of the updated post-war T–6G version to bring total production to over 20,000. These trainers could be fitted with light bomb racks and a fixed machine-gun in either or both wing roots, plus another manually operated gun in the rear cockpit, originally for bombing and gunnery training although in recent years armament has been used for counter-insurgency (COIN) operations rather than training; the RAF used armed Harvards against the Mau Mau in Kenya and the Malayan terrorists. The Brazilian Air Force until recently used some 90 T–6Gs for COIN duties, as do several African air forces, and AT–6s or Harvards were supplied after the war to over 50 different countries, more than 2,000 being refurbished by North American alone for post-war export.

Among the types for which large orders had been placed in 1939–40 both by Britain and France was the Curtiss P–40 fighter, named Tomahawk by the RAF, which purchased 140 Tomahawk Is, IAs and IBs outright (some being taken over from French contracts) and 1,041 Tomahawk IIs later; nearly 300 of the Mk IIs were diverted to China for the American Volunteer Group and to Russia. Anxious that P–40 deliveries should not fall behind because of insufficient production capacity, the British Purchasing Commission had first discussed with North American's executives in the autumn of 1939 the possibility of their building the Curtiss P–40 under licence as a second source of production, and had revived this idea in January 1940. This prospect did not appeal greatly to the company's president, J. H. 'Dutch' Kindelberger, who had been following closely the accounts of the air war in Europe and who had already conceived in broad outline the fighter that was to become the Mustang. It was suggested that North American be permitted to submit the design of a new type of fighter, incorporating all the latest aerodynamic refinements and the operational experience of air combat since the beginning of the war, to meet the Purchasing Commission's requirements.

By April 1940 the Commission considered the Curtiss P–40 as unsuitable for European combat conditions and was in need of a substitute, so it agreed to North American's suggestion to submit its own design to the Commission's requirements, with one very important stipulation—that in view of the serious war situation (Denmark and Norway had been invaded on 9 April) a prototype must be completed within 120 days. After

The silver North American NA–73X prototype shows its very clean lines in an early flight (*RIC*)

discussions with the Commission in New York Mr Kindelberger sent a telegram alerting North American's design engineers on 24 April. The design team, headed by Raymond H. Rice, vice-president in charge of engineering, and chief designer Edgar Schmued, a naturalised US citizen born in Bavaria who had served in the Austrian Air Service in World War I, worked right through the night to produce for Kindelberger the preliminary general arrangement drawings of the North American NA–73X, as the new fighter was designated. After sending his telegram Kindelberger had left for California, and the g.a. drawings were airmailed to his colleague, first vice-president J. L. Atwood, who was continuing discussions with the Commission and presented them with the g.a. drawings. The Commission liked what they saw, and on the basis of the drawings an initial order for 320 of the new fighters was placed, dated 29 May 1940, at a price later fixed at $50,000 per aircraft; a second order for 300 was placed before the first flight took place.

This was very gratifying, for North American's only previous attempt at a fighter had been the NA–50A (or NA–68) designed in 1939 for Thailand; this was essentially a more powerful single-seat development of the Harvard/Texan trainer, with an 875hp Wright R–1820–77 Cyclone nine-cylinder radial engine. The six NA–68s destined for the Royal Thai Air Force were on board ship at Hawaii on their way to Thailand when Japanese forces entered that country; they were seized by the US government and turned over to the USAAF under the designation P–64. They were used as advanced fighter trainers for training American and Chinese cadets; in their original form armament was two 20mm cannon in underwing fairings and two 0·303in machine-guns firing over the engine cowling, and two 100lb bombs or one 550lb bomb could be carried externally.

In view of North American's lack of previous fighter design experience the Commission had insisted that the company buy some Curtiss P–40 wind tunnel data from the Curtiss–Wright Corporation. But the NA–73 was in fact far more advanced aerodynamically in concept than the P–40, and with the same Allison V–1710 engine, far outperformed the Curtiss fighter. The NA–73 was one of the first fighters to have a laminar flow wing, with a specially shaped aerofoil section with its maximum thickness well aft to maintain as far as possible laminar flow, or air flow parallel with the wing surface over which it passed. On a conventional wing this is difficult to maintain because of the boundary layer near the surface which moves more slowly than the rest and breaks away in turbulence, thus increasing drag. The NA–73's wing section had been evolved by North American from NACA (National Advisory Committee for Aeronautics) laminar low-drag theory, research data and wind tunnel results, and it gave greatly reduced drag that was to be a major factor in the Mustang's outstanding performance, in particular its great range.

The idea of using the then new laminar flow wing was not part of the original concept of the new fighter, and had been proposed by Ed Horkey, who later recalled that several North American aerodynamicists and technical personnel were virtual prisoners in a smoke-filled room for more than a week calculating the ordinates which determine the wing section and laying out the wing; one or two NACA personnel, such as Russ Robinson, who had recently been appointed in charge of NACA's West Coast Liaison Office, were willingly press-ganged into helping on the all-important aerofoil design. This was, in fact, a wholly original section created by North American for the NA–73 and not, as is often stated, a modification by the firm of an existing NACA laminar flow section.

Some idea of the performance the laminar flow wing made possible was given by Paul Mantz in the 1947 Bendix Trophy Race when he flew his red P–51C–10–NT Mustang NX1202 into first place non-stop over the 2,048-mile course from Van Nuys, California, to Cleveland, Ohio, at the staggering *average* speed of 460·423mph; second place was taken by Joe DeBona in a P–51D, who finished only 78 seconds behind Mantz. Admittedly Mantz, who flew the course at 20,000–30,000ft to take advantage of the best winds, was using a specially prepared racing aircraft wet-sanded, waxed and polished all over to a mirror-smooth finish and a highly-boosted Packard-Merlin engine (reports say that he used up to 105 inches of mercury for boost), and so his performance could not be taken as typical of production Mustangs in squadron service. But it does highlight the type's exceptional combination of speed and range that made it such a good long-range escort fighter.

The second distinctive drag-reducing feature of the NA–73 was the location of the radiator air intake underneath the centre/rear fuselage, thus enabling the fuselage cross-section to be kept to the minimum depth and a very cleanly-cowled nose to be achieved. The radiator scoop had a forward and a rear shutter that were thermostatically-controlled, the cooling air providing a small amount of extra thrust as it passed out of the rear shutter. Normally, heat energy passing into a radiator from the engine is wasted, but if, as on the NA–73, the air is made to enter a properly contoured duct and is allowed to expand and slow down at the radiator, it will pick up heat from the radiator itself and eject from the rear shutter at a higher velocity and increased thrust. But when North American first tested a model of the radiator intake in the California Institute of Technology low speed wind tunnel it looked as if the whole concept might have to be redesigned, as the airflow was not slowing down through the radiator as it should have done. The problem was eventually traced to interference with the fuselage boundary layer, and a small boundary layer 'splitter gap' was left between the top of the radiator inlet scoop and the bottom of the fuselage, the scoop being about three inches away from the fuselage so as to give the optimum combination of minimum drag with best internal flow through the radiator and heat transfer therefrom. The coolant itself was a 30/70 mixture of ethylene-glycol and water; the double radiator unit, which was secured by two metal straps to the underside of the fuselage, consisted, on the Allison versions, of a circular inner honeycomb cell for oil cooling surrounded by an outer circular cell for the glycol. On the more powerful Merlin-engined versions the radiator intake was deepened and the radiator assembly was square, with a separate oil radiator.

It is interesting to note that the Curtiss P–40, in its prototype XP–40 form, initially had a similarly positioned coolant radiator

to the NA–73, but this was later moved forward to under the XP–40's nose, and from the P–40D and subsequent versions was moved further forward to just behind the airscrew.

North American also influenced propeller design for the Mustang, and its aerodynamicists enjoyed a close relationship with the technical personnel in Hamilton Standard and Aeroproducts, so that the firm was able to specify the blade plan forms and aerofoil sections and other aspects of airscrew design to get the maximum thrust from the horsepower developed.

Another distinctive feature of the NA–73's appearance were the square-cut wings and tail surfaces; these simplified production and had virtually no effect on performance, although they did give the Mustang a strong resemblance to the Messerschmitt Bf 109E. During the war a popular legend had it that the reason for this likeness was that North American's chief designer Edgar Schmued had once spent several years in the Messerschmitt drawing office, but he had left Europe in 1925 and had never had any association with the German firm.

It was a remarkable tribute to the basic structural simplicity and ease of production of the Mustang that it required only 200 more man-hours of labour to build than the AT–6 Texan/Harvard trainer. And compared with three other major US fighter types, the Lockheed P–38K Lightning, the Republic P–47D Thunderbolt and the Bell P–63A Kingcobra, the P–51D Mustang was the cheapest to produce, with a total cost of $58,546 compared with $66,010 for the P–63A and $115,434 for the P–47D. The Thunderbolt's massive airframe, at $65,308, was more than twice as costly as the P–51D's at $26,600.

Meanwhile great efforts were being made to meet the Purchasing Commission's very tight schedule of 120 days for the completion of the prototype. Production of detail design drawings had begun on 5 May and by great efforts the company-funded NA–73X prototype, bearing the civil registration NX19998, was pushed out of the assembly hangar on 30 August, or 117 days after detail design work had started; it had wheels borrowed from an AT–6 trainer and was without an engine, the 1,150hp (maxi-

The prototype NA–73X on its back after the fifth flight on 20 November 1940 for airspeed calibration had resulted in a forced landing at Inglewood; the pilot, Paul Balfour, escaped uninjured (*RIC*)

mum take-off) Allison V–1710–F3R (or V–1710–39, to give it its military designation) being late in delivery. Allison was in fact going through a period of production delays with the V–1710 engine, and found itself temporarily unable to meet the demand caused by the large orders for V–1710–powered types such as the Curtiss P–40, Bell P–39 Airacobra and Lockheed P–38 Lightning. At one time in the autumn of 1940 there were dozens of Curtiss P–40s and Tomahawks standing idle at the Curtiss Buffalo plant awaiting delivery of their V–1710 engines. North American had to wait some six weeks for the prototype's engine to arrive, and after several modifications had been made, the prototype made its first flight on 26 October 1940 piloted by Vance Breeze, the chief test pilot.

The first few flights were successful, apart from a tendency for the Allison V–1710 to overheat, but on the fifth flight, on 20 November, the engine cut out as a result of a fuel switching error, and in the crash that followed, the prototype turned over on to its back. Luckily it was not seriously damaged and the pilot, Paul Balfour, was

The prototype NA–73X is righted after its accident, showing the 'experimental' category registration NX19998 on the starboard wing (*RIC*)

rescued uninjured by North American personnel, who had to dig away the ground underneath the aircraft to allow the sideways-hingeing cockpit canopy to be opened and the pilot to be extricated. The flight

test programme disclosed very few snags and North American's achievement in meeting the almost impossible schedule of 120 days for prototype completion set by the Purchasing Commission was all the more creditable in view of the firm's almost complete lack of previous fighter design experience; this was a time-scale matched by few, if any, other fighters of comparable complexity and performance.

With no significant modifications made necessary by the flight test programme, production was able to start almost at once, at first on a fairly small scale to meet the RAF orders as, with the Cash and Carry arrangements still in force, military hardware for Britain had to be purchased in cash or acquired through barter deals. But by December 1940 the UK could no longer continue to buy American military equipment at the rate it had been doing as its dollar reserves were almost used up; an alternative trading arrangement had to be found for future purchases, and President Roosevelt and his administration, aware of this problem, had been working their way towards a solution for several months. At this distance in time we tend to take Lend-Lease, the concept devised to solve that

Mustang I AG346 was the first to be delivered to Britain, arriving at Speke Airport, Liverpool, in November 1941; note serial repeated in very small letters on the rudder (*RIC*)

problem, rather for granted as a part of history; there have, after all, been many other instances of American generosity since then in aid of one kind or another to other countries. But, at the time, Lend-Lease was a startlingly bold proposal completely without precedent in that its essence was to provide unlimited aid to Britain or any other of America's allies, without any strings attached.

The Lend-Lease Bill, introduced into the House of Representatives on 10 January 1941, authorised the President to 'sell, transfer title to, exchange, lease, lend or otherwise dispose of . . . any defence article' to any country whose defence the President deemed 'vital to the defence of the United States'. Payment or repayment for such defence material might be, to quote the Bill, 'payment or repayment in kind or property, or any other direct or indirect benefit which the President deems satisfactory'. In other words, there was no question of a nation's assets in the States being confiscated, or similar reprisal action

The tenth production aircraft, serialled 41–39, which was the second of two XP–51s delivered free to the US Army Air Corps for evaluation at Wright Field (*RIC*)

being taken if, through force of circumstances (such as German occupation) it found itself unable to pay in hard cash for American military equipment it had acquired; a satisfactory settlement could be made eventually. The Lend-Lease Bill became law when it was signed by the President on 11 March 1941 and thereafter Mustangs for the RAF were ordered by the Americans and allotted to Britain.

The RAF named the new fighter 'Mustang' after the wild horses common to California and Mexico, and the first production aircraft with the RAF serial AG345, made its first flight on 16 April 1941; it was retained by North American for flight development. The second production aircraft, AG346, was shipped over to Britain and delivered to Speke Airport, Liverpool, in November 1941, being the first of the type to arrive in Britain; it went straight to the A & AEE at Boscombe Down. Armament of the Mustang I was two 0·5in Browning MG 53–2 machine-guns mounted below the engine each side of the crankcase and firing through the airscrew disc, and one 0·5in MG 53 and two 0·3in MG 40 machine-guns in each wing. When design of the NA–73 had begun, the US authorities had stipulated only that two examples should be delivered free to the USAAF for evaluation if the NA–73 went into production. Accordingly the fourth and tenth production aircraft were given the serials 41–38 and 41–39 and went to Wright Field for testing by the USAAF, who designated them XP–51s. They achieved the very high maximum speed of 382mph, which was faster than almost every other fighter then flying, and these XP–51s had a gross weight of 8,400lb. After very successful trials with them the USAAF placed an order for 150 production P–51s under the name Apache, which was later changed to Mustang to standardise with the RAF, and this order was later followed by one for 310 P–51As. The P–51 differed from the Mustang I chiefly in having four 20mm M–2 cannon in the wings; the P–51 also had leakproof fuel tanks.

Technical description

The Mustang's exceptional performance was achieved by an airframe of conventional all-metal stressed skin construction. The

15

wing, of 5 degrees dihedral, was made in two sections that were bolted together on the fuselage centre-line, the upper wing surface forming the cockpit floor. The wing itself was a two-spar structure with smooth Alclad skin, the spars having single plate flanges with extruded top and bottom booms. Pressed ribs with flanged lightening holes and extruded spanwise stringers completed the basic wing structure. The ailerons and single-slotted, hydraulically operated flaps were hinged on the rear spar, the ailerons being metal-covered with a controllable trim tab in the port one. The post-war Trans-Florida Cavalier executive/ private owner version of the Mustang had a trim tab in each aileron, as well as a step in each flap to facilitate entry to the cockpit. Self-sealing non-metallic fuel cells or tanks of 92 US gallons capacity each were installed between the spars, one in each wing, and there was a structural door provided in the underside of each wing for removal and installation of these cells. Many P–51Bs and P–51Cs were fitted with a self-sealing 85 US gal fuel tank in the fuselage behind the pilot, bringing the total internal fuel capacity to 269 US gal, and with the P–51D this tank became standard.

The oval-section fuselage was built in three main sections, the engine section, the main section and the tail section, and was

The fifth of 150 P–51s ordered by the USAAF under the name Apache; these had four 20mm M–2 cannon (*RIC*)

constructed entirely of Alclad and aluminium alloy extrusions, except for the cockpit armour. The engine section consisted of two V-type cantilever engine bearers on the Allison-powered versions built up of plate webs and top and bottom extruded members, each attached at two points to the front fireproof bulkhead of the main section. The latter consisted of two beams, each side beam comprising two longerons, which formed the caps, and the skin, reinforced by vertical frames, forming the webs. Aft of the cockpit the longerons extended into a semi-monocoque structure reinforced by vertical frames, and the detachable tail section continued the structure of the rear portion of the main section. The cockpit canopy was at first sideways-hingeing, but the bulged, rearward-sliding, frameless Malcolm canopy was fitted to many P–51Bs and Cs and Mustang IIIs after their arrival in Britain, and the P–51D and subsequent versions featured the large moulded plastic 'bubble'-type sliding canopy for still further improved rear vision. The windshield incorporated an optically flat 5-ply laminated glass bullet-proof front panel with side panels of safety glass. There were two plates of case-hardened steel armour behind the pilot's seat, and there was also a crash pylon behind the pilot. Radio and oxygen were provided for the pilot, as well as cockpit heating and ventilation; the electrical system was a 24-volt one. On the Allison-powered versions, which had a down-draught induction system, the carburettor intake with ice guard was located above the cowling, whereas on the Merlin-engined versions this intake was moved to below the nose to cater for the Merlin's up-draught induction system; the ventral radiator intake was deepened and the coolant radiator itself was of square section instead of the circular section of Allison versions. There was an oil tank of 12 US gal capacity in the engine compartment on the firewall.

The fin and tailplane structure comprised two spars, pressed ribs and extruded stringers, the whole covered with stressed Alclad skin. The one-piece tailplane had detachable tips, and both rudder and elevators were fabric-covered over aluminium alloy frames. These control surfaces were dynamically balanced, with a plastic rudder trim tab and plywood elevator tabs. Later production P–51Ds were fitted with a dorsal fin to compensate for the reduction of side area through the cutting down of the rear fuselage, and this fin was also fitted retrospectively to many of the earlier Ds; the P–51H had a much shallower dorsal fin.

The inwards-retracting main wheels and legs were accommodated forward of the main spar, the undercarriage track being 11ft 10in. The cantilever air-oil shock absorber legs were hinged to large forged fittings bolted to reinforced wing ribs. Retraction was hydraulic and the fairing plates on the undercarriage legs and the inner wheel doors formed part of the wing contour over the main undercarriage when it was retracted. The main wheel brakes were hydraulic, and the forwards-retracting tailwheel was fully swivelling and steerable within the range of rudder pedal travel.

The Allison's limitations

Tests at Boscombe Down with the first Mustang to arrive in Britain had soon shown the type to be a very good fighter—far better, in fact, than any of the previous American fighters—but for one shortcom-

ing: the low-rated altitude of its Allison V–1710–39 engine, which gave 1,000hp at 12,000ft, led to a lack of performance at height that restricted its usefulness for many of a fighter's normal duties, such as interception or escort, in spite of the single-stage, single-speed supercharger fitted to this version of the engine. The Allison V–1710 was, in fact, America's sole representative of the large, 12-cylinder, liquid-cooled in-line engine on the outbreak of war, and by the time it flew in the NA–73 prototype its basic design was already ten years old, older than its contemporary, the Rolls-Royce Merlin, but it had not been developed to the same extent. America had neglected the big in-line engine in the 1930s in favour of the radial, especially the Pratt & Whitney Wasp range and the Wright Whirlwind and Cyclone series, and even their specialist racing aircraft built for the Bendix Trophy or Thompson Trophy, like the Granville Gee-Bee, almost always had radials. Whereas for Britain, racing experience in the shape of the Schneider Trophy contests, which led to the magnificent Rolls-Royce 'R' engine, fed directly into the mainstream of fighter and engine development, in the States it tended to be much more separated from it, and to produce dangerous 'hot rods' like the Granville Gee-Bee Super Sportster. This, although very fast—it broke the world's landplane speed record in 1932 at 294·2mph—was unstable about all three axes and could only be flown by an experienced pilot. So although the last Schneider Trophy contest was in 1931 and the Bendix and Thompson Trophy races in the States were flown up to 1940 when the war called a halt to them, paradoxically enough air racing exerted far less influence on US fighter development than on British, and it was the Merlin-engined Mustang that returned after the war to dominate the US racing scene.

But having said that, a little-known fact must be recorded, that one of the leading racing pilots in the States, Art Chester, played an important part in the Mustang success story as the man in charge of powerplant design and installation. Art had started air racing back in 1923 and throughout the 1920s and 1930s had not only won many races but built up a vast experience of tuning high-performance racing engines and getting more power out of them; his Chester Special which he flew in the National Air Races of 1933 in Los Angeles was designed and built by himself, and powered by a Menasco engine which he had supercharged and tuned to increase its power from 125hp to 200hp. He continued to build and race his own aircraft after joining the Menasco engine company in 1936, and when war broke out and it was clear that the days of racing were numbered, he applied for a job at North American, at first as an engineering test pilot. Instead, he was hired for his engine expertise and put in charge of the engine installation of the little two-seat NA–35 primary trainer powered by a 165hp Menasco Pirate C4S–2 in-line engine; only four of these were built in the end. In April 1940, when the NA–73 got under way, Chester did a similar job, being responsible for everything forward of the cockpit, and his experience with racing engines proved to be invaluable. After the war Art returned to racing, playing a leading part in the field of the Goodyear Trophy Formula 1 midget racers, which had an engine capacity limited to 190cu in. Tragically, he was killed on 24 April 1949 at San Diego in a second heat Formula 1 race when his 'Swee' Pea II', which had a butterfly tail, went into a high speed stall, snap-rolled and crashed inverted.

Prior to the Allison V–1710, America had produced some very good in-line engines in the 1920s; Sir Richard (then Mr C. R.) Fairey had been so impressed by the Curtiss D–12 engine on a visit to the States in 1923 that he selected it as the powerplant for the Fairey Fox single-engined bomber. This, when it appeared in 1925, was faster than any contemporary fighter and 50mph faster than any other RAF bomber then in service, owing to the finely streamlined nose cowling permitted by the Curtiss engine (built by Fairey as the Felix). Only one RAF squadron—No 12—was equipped with the Fox, although 178 were built by Avions Fairey in Belgium for that country's air force.

Mustang Is in action
Although the Mustang I's performance fell off at height, it was a sparkling performer

Mustang Is AG550: U–XV and AM112: X–XV of the first Mustang squadron, No 2 at Sawbridgeworth, in 1942 (*IWM*)

at lower altitudes, having a maximum speed of 390mph at 8,000ft. This made it an excellent choice for the Tac R or tactical reconnaissance role, and so Mustang Is were fitted in Britain with a single F.24 or K.24 camera mounted obliquely behind the pilot's seat facing through the port rear vision panel; the K.24 was a US-built version of the British F.24 camera constructed under licence, and both the K.24 and F.24 took a 5in square picture. The camera was sighted by bringing the object to be photographed in line with a mark on the wing trailing edge, which obviated the need for flying straight and level and thus presenting an easier target for anti-aircraft fire. By this means a well-defended target could be photographed from a reasonable distance or an easier one from an almost vertical bank over the target. The Mustang I began to take over the Tac R role in Army Co-operation Command from the Curtiss P-40 Tomahawk, and the first RAF unit to equip with it was No 2 Squadron at Sawbridgeworth in Hertfordshire, not far from Bishop's Stortford, in April 1942. The Mustang's first operational sortie was made on 10 May 1942 and other squadrons soon began re-equipping with the type; Mustangs of No 39 Wing, from Nos 26, 238, 400 and 414 Squadrons, took a major part in the Dieppe raid on 19 August, supporting the troops on the ground and encountering their first Bf 109s. This costly raid, intended to gain experience in landing on an enemy coast, was the first large combined operation in which air, land and naval forces participated, and nine Mustangs were lost during the operation. The Army Co-operation Mustangs usually flew their sorties in pairs, all the aircraft of a particular squadron crossing the English coast at one spot, crossing the Channel at sea level to avoid detection by German radar, and then each pair would spread out fanwise to their allotted targets. The leader of each pair would take his photos after climbing to around 900ft with his wing man guarding his tail.

A notable flight from northern Scotland to Norway and back was made on 27 September 1942 by a Mustang I of a Polish squadron, No 309, flown by Fl Lt J. Lewkowicz—acting without orders and on his own initiative. This unit was equipped with Lysanders until June, when the first Mustangs arrived for No 309's 'B' Flight; the squadron had long wanted something more modern than the elderly Westland monoplane, which still equipped 'A' and 'C' flights, and while they waited and during the working-up period on Mustangs Lewkowicz, a fully qualified engineer, had made carefully-checked calculations of the optimum fuel consumption, boost pressure settings and rpm of the Mustang which showed that it could fly to Norway and back. He had sent his calculations to Group Headquarters but had not received a reply, and so decided to prove the correctness of his figures and to draw attention to them at the same time by setting out for Stavanger, where he attacked enemy positions in the area and flew home safely to his base at Dalcross, some 10 miles from Inverness, after a round trip of some 700 miles. He was reprimanded for acting without orders, but at the same time warmly congratulated and highly commended by the AOC, Air Marshal Sir Arthur Barratt, and as a result of this flight RAF Mustang squadrons began to attack more distant targets. No 309 itself in May 1943 moved to Snailwell, near Newmarket in Berkshire, from where it flew recce sorties over the Dutch ports and ranged as far as the Frisian Islands. Mustangs of other RAF squadrons were frequently used on cross-Channel sweeps, attacking ground targets as well as taking photos, and these units did a good deal of the photo-reconnaissance necessary before the D-Day landings to build up a detailed picture of the German defences. Mustang Is had been the first single-engined UK-based fighters to penetrate German airspace when on 21 October 1942 they had made an attack on the Dortmund-Ems canal; after machine-gunning a military camp from tree-top height on the way they shot up some barges on the canal.

Apart from No 2 Squadron, which had also been the first unit to re-equip with the Curtiss P-40 Tomahawk in August 1941 when these fighters began to replace the Westland Lysanders for tactical reconnaissance, the following squadrons used Mustang Is, IAs and IIs: Nos 4, 13, 16, 26, 63, 116, 168, 225, 239, 241, 268, 309, 315, 400, 414, 430, and 613. The RAF's 620 Mustang Is, with serials AG345–AG664, AL958–AM257

and AP164–AP263, were paid for as Cash and Carry aircraft, the first to be supplied under Lend-Lease being 150 Mustang IAs, serialled FD418–FD567, which differed from the Mk I in having four 20mm M–2 cannon in the wings replacing the eight 0·5in and 0·3in machine-guns. But 57 of these were retained for service with the USAAF and conversion to F–6A photo recce variants, later being designated P–51–1s. Several Mustang Is were used for various test or trial installations jobs, especially of armament: AG393 was used at the RAE, Farnborough, for drag tests on camouflage paint, and AG357/G was fitted with eight 60lb rocket projectiles under the wings. AM130 also had rocket projectiles under the wings, while AM106/G was fitted successively with eight rocket projectiles on zero-length launchers, then with special long-range fuel tanks and finally with two 40mm Vickers 'S' cannon in fairings under the wings. This gun was also fitted to the Hurricane IID for tank-busting, but it was a heavy piece of armament and rocket projectiles found much more favour for the ground attack role, although they were not usually used by RAF Mustangs in squadron

Mustang 1 AG357/G used for a trial installation of eight 60lb rocket projectiles under the wings (*BR*)

service. AM190 was retained in the United States in USAAF markings for the prototype four-cannon installation of the P–51, but the great majority of both RAF and USAAF Mustangs had machine-gun armament, whereas most other fighters, having started with machine-guns, went over to cannon-equipped versions.

An interesting 'one-off' modification was the fitting of a Mustang with a Maclaren drift undercarriage; Alan Muntz & Co Ltd at Heston Airport had done the design work for this installation. This type of undercarriage was first proposed in 1938 by O. F. Maclaren as a means of overcoming the difficulty of landing with an adverse crosswind component and also, by allowing aircraft so equipped to land on a particular runway almost regardless of the wind direction, to enable a major airport's cost to be far cheaper because fewer runways would be required. The principle of this undercarriage was that the wheels could be set at the angle of drift, so that although the aircraft was 'crabbing' the wheels were

This underneath view of a Mustang 1A shows its four 20mm M–2 cannon (*IWM*)

parallel to the flight path and set at an angle to the aircraft's longitudinal axis, instead of parallel to it as with a normal landing gear. The Maclaren undercarriage was first fitted to the Arpin A–1 two-seat pusher lightplane, which had a nosewheel undercarriage, before the war and was fairly successful. The war put a stop to further development for a time, but the idea was revived by Airwork Ltd at Heston and the undercarriage was fitted experimentally to a Miles M.14A Magister trainer and an Airspeed Oxford before being tried on the Mustang. In the Magister installation the wheels and oleo legs were turned mechanically, while on the Oxford the wheels were moved by hydraulic operation, and could be set at an angle of 25 degrees to the longitudinal axis. In the Mustang, the wheel-setting mechanism was mounted behind each oleo shock-absorber. These trial installations of the Maclaren gear produced satisfactory results on the whole, and had this concept been developed more energetically at an earlier date many of the post-war trials and tribu-

lations of London Heathrow, which in its original form had six runways with the terminal buildings misguidedly sited in the centre of them to the detriment of future expansion, might have been avoided.

As mentioned earlier, the USAAF had ordered 150 P–51s under the name Apache, later changed to Mustang, and, with four 20mm M–2 cannon, these corresponded to the RAF Mustang IA. Rather surprisingly, these were not used operationally, although with its exceptional range for a fighter the P–51 would have been just the job for the Pacific war. One F–6A, or rather P–51–1 reconnaissance version, was painted in an experimental black and white dazzle or 'splinter'-type colour scheme, not unlike the kind of paint schemes applied both to merchant ships and warships since World War I days, the idea of this being to break up the ship's outline and make it look to a watching U-boat as if it was heading in a different direction and at a different speed to the actual course. This P–51–1, painted with a sort of zebra stripe effect, even had its national insignia deleted, and had an oblique camera mounted in a blister fairing at the rear of the cockpit.

The next USAAF version was the P–51A, of which 310 were ordered and which differed from the P–51 chiefly in armament, having four 0·5in Browning MG 53 machine-guns in the wings. This was the first variant with underwing bomb racks, which could take either two 500lb bombs or two 75 or 150 US gal drop tanks; with the latter the P–51A had a ferrying range of no less than 2,350 miles and a maximum loaded weight of 10,600lb. Later production P–51As had the more powerful Allison V–1710–81 engine (civil designation V–1710–F20R) which gave 1,200hp for take-off, and was rated at 1,125hp at 15,500ft. The RAF equivalent of the P–51A was the Mustang II, fifty of which were delivered late in 1942 serialled FR890–FR939. This also had the V–1710–81 engine as an alternative to the earlier V–1710–39, and most Mustang IIs went to join Mk Is and IAs in RAF squadrons. One, FR901, was fitted experimentally with two big 'trouser'-shaped fuel tanks of deep section under the wings for ultra-long-range sorties or ferrying, but these tanks were not adopted, as the Mustang's conventional drop tanks gave it sufficient range.

The USAAF also used the Mustang in the tactical reconnaissance role, a total of fifty-seven Mustang IAs originally destined for the RAF being retained and converted in 1942 to have two K.24 cameras; they were provisionally redesignated F–6As but later

The P–51A seen here differed from the P–51 only in armament, having four 0·5in Browning MG 53 machine-guns in place of the cannon (*RIC*)

became known as P–51–1s. Unlike the RAF's Tac R Mustangs, the F–6A or P–51–1 was unarmed, and it had a gross weight of 8,900lb. The F–6B, of which thirty-five were produced, was a similar conversion of the P–51A, and some F–6Bs were later fitted with the Malcolm bulged sliding cockpit canopy for better rear vision that was featured on the P–51B and P–51C.

The first version of the Mustang actually to see combat service with the USAAF was not, as might have been expected, the P–51 or P–51A, but the A–36A–NA, a dive-bomber version of the P–51A evolved in the spring of 1942 which went into action in Sicily and Italy in 1943, equipping two groups. This was fitted with hydraulically operated wing-mounted air brakes, one above and one below each wing outboard of the bomb racks which, when closed, lay in recesses flush with the normal wing surface. This air brake installation made the A–36A heavier than the P–51A and reduced its maximum speed to 356mph; the dive brakes were not particularly satisfactory in operation and were eventually wired shut. Armament was six 0·5in Browning MG 53 machine-guns, four in the wings and two mounted beside the engine as on the Mustang I. Powerplant of the A–36A was the 1,325hp (maximum take-off) Allison

This A–36A–NA dive-bomber version of the P–51A has the dive brakes above and below the wings extended; these dive brakes proved to be troublesome and were later wired shut (*RIC*)

One A–36A serialled EW998 was supplied to the RAF for evaluation, and is seen here with dive brakes open carrying two 500lb bombs under the wings (*IWM*)

V–1710–87 (or V–1710–F21R) engine. The A–36A first flew in September 1942 and production ended in March 1943 with a total of 500 built. It was unofficially named Invader later in 1943, but reverted to Mustang, and the name Invader was afterwards given to the Douglas A–26 attack bomber. One A–36A, serialled EW998, was

A few A–36As were painted in German markings to represent Messerschmitt Bf 109Es for the Warner Brothers film *Fighter Squadron* (*HH*)

supplied to the RAF in March 1943 for evaluation, and was used for bombing trials.

The dive bomber's star was already on the wane when the A–36A was conceived, for although types such as the Douglas SBD Dauntless had been used to excellent effect by the US Navy in the Battles of the Coral Sea and Midway, the heavy losses suffered by the dreaded Junkers Ju 87 Stuka during the Battle of Britain had made it plain that, in the European and other theatres of war, the specialist dive bomber could only operate with adequate fighter cover or where there was only inadequate opposition. From 1941 onwards, more and more fighter types were modified to carry bombs, and later rocket projectiles, and these made dive bombers such as the Stuka obsolete. The A–36A was an unusual instance of trying—with the aid of air brakes—to turn an existing fighter back into an old-style dive bomber, and its concept suggests that USAAF official thinking had yet to recognise the Mustang's true potentialities. A–36As were sometimes used for bomber escort in Italy, and on a few occasions they dropped food and medical supplies to troops in forward positions.

2 Merlin Metamorphosis

It soon became clear that the Mustang was far too good a fighter to spend the rest of the war limited to the tactical reconnaissance or other essentially low-level roles because of the performance limitations at height of its Allison V–1710 engine. With this powerplant its manoeuvrability and speed were excellent, far superior to the Spitfire V, and its fine performance between 10,000ft and 20,000ft was good, although with the low-rated Allison it fell off above this height. But the V–1710 had not been developed to the same extent as the Merlin, especially in supercharged high-altitude versions, and in some ways it was not a wholly satisfactory engine; not only did the performance leave something to be desired but for North American's president, J. H. 'Dutch' Kindelberger, and his colleagues there was the memory of how late delivery of the V–1710 for the prototype NA–73 had delayed its first flight by some six weeks and spoilt the very tight schedule they were working to to meet the British Purchasing Commission's requirements. At a meeting at Wright Field in 1943 with E. O. Hunt, executive vice-president of General Motors, of which Allison was a division, Kindelberger spelt out in detail the technical reasons why his company would be staying with the Rolls-Royce Merlin for future versions of the Mustang, and mentioned the fact that Packard as the Merlin manufacturers would always work with them on any technical solution they requested to a problem involving the minimum of drag. By contrast, an Allison solution to a spark plug wiring problem in the V–1710 had involved a bulge in the engine cowling that destroyed its minimum drag profile, and there was a feeling that perhaps Allison, with their monopoly of big in-line engine production in the States until Packard began building the Merlin, were not as customer-orientated as they should have been.

With no high-altitude version of the V–1710 available at the stage of the Mustang's entry into RAF service in 1942, the question arose of an alternative powerplant, and several people began to arrive at the conclusion that the Rolls-Royce Merlin, especially in its new high-altitude Mk 61 form with two-stage two-speed supercharger and intercooler, was the engine the Mustang needed to realise its full potential. The first person to do so was Rolls-Royce test pilot Ron Harker, whose job it was to fly Rolls-powered aircraft in use by the Services in the field, see how their engines were performing, give advice on technical problems and generally act as a trouble-shooter, and also to fly aircraft powered by Rolls-Royce's competitors and rivals, including German types if the opportunity arose. In the course of this work he was invited down to the Air Fighting Development Unit at Duxford to fly an Allison-engined Mustang I, and after spending thirty minutes flying AG422 on 30 April 1942, left very impressed with its low and medium altitude performance. Back at Hucknall his thoughts began to turn to the Merlin 61 for the Mustang; at the beginning of 1942 this engine had been fitted to a standard Spitfire Vc to produce one of the prototype Spitfire IXs, and this had increased its maximum speed by 44mph at 28,000ft to 417mph. This showed what was possible, and the Merlin 65 and 66 coming along had superchargers geared for maximum performance at low altitudes.

Harker contacted the Chief Aerodynamic Engineer at Rolls-Royce's Flight Development Establishment at Hucknall, Mr W. O. W. Challier, and asked him to work out some estimated performance figures for a Mustang powered by the Merlin 61 (at that time the only version in the high altitude 60-series of Merlins available), with figures for a Merlin XX-powered version for comparison; the Mk XX with a single-stage two-speed supercharger was in production for the Beaufighter II, Defiant, and several marks of the Halifax, Lancaster and Hurricane. On 8 June 1942 Challier presented his report, which gave the top speed of the hypothetical Merlin XX Mustang as 400mph at 18,600ft, but with the Merlin 61 the maximum speed leapt dramatically to 441mph at 25,600ft. With the support of R. N. Dorey, the Manager at Hucknall, Harker went direct to E. W. Hives (later Lord Hives), the Director and General

Works Manager of Rolls-Royce at Derby, to acquaint him with the possibilities of a Merlin 61-engined Mustang and to see if an aircraft could be obtained for conversion. Hives was persuaded by Harker's recommendations and Challier's figures, and the idea of converting the Mustang to take the Merlin was approved.

Interest in the re-engined fighter began to grow, with the RAF considering it as additional to the Spitfire IX and VIII, and there was already American interest; the US air attaché in London, Lt-Colonel Thomas Hitchcock, was well known at Rolls-Royce and aware of the latest developments there, and his attitude to the Merlin 61 Mustang was very enthusiastic. In the summer of 1942 he reported to Washington that fitting the Merlin to the Mustang would produce the finest all-round fighter the Allies could wish for, and he advised its development as a high-altitude fighter by installing the Merlin 61. This view was soon to be endorsed by such influential people as Air Chief Marshal Sir Trafford Leigh-Mallory, then AOC-in-C Fighter Command, and Captain Eddie Rickenbacker, but it was Hitchcock's enthusiasm that provided the necessary bridge between British acceptance of the Merlin Mustang's potentialities and American approval, and which did so much to pave the way for large-scale production of the P–51B and later variants. Sadly, Hitchcock was killed in 1944 when the pro-

AL975/G was the first of five Mustang 1s fitted with Merlin 65 engines and redesignated Mustang Xs, and first flew in this form on 13 October 1942. The intake below the cowling was deeper on these Mustangs to accommodate the intercooler radiator, whose air exit louvres can be seen in the cowling just over the wing leading edge. Seen here as refitted with a Merlin 70 engine and increased fin chord, AL975 has now lost the '/G' from its serial (*RR*)

duction P–51 he was flying broke up in the air near Salisbury.

Six weeks after his first report of the performance of the Mustang powered by the Merlin XX and 61, Challier sent out a revised set of figures based on Mustang AG518, which was shortly grounded to enable Rolls-Royce technicians and engineers to study how best the Merlin 61 could be installed. These figures were further revised when it was decided to substitute a new 11ft 4in diameter propeller with a reduction gear ratio of 0·42 to 1, specially designed for the Merlin Mustang, for the Spitfire IX-type 10ft 9in diameter four-blade Jablo airscrew with a reduction gear ratio of 0·477 to 1 originally proposed. Final figures for the Merlin 61 version with the new propeller at an all-up weight of 9,100lb showed a maximum speed at sea level of 345mph in MS gear (Medium Supercharger) and a maximum speed at full throttle height (that height at which an aircraft attains its fastest speed at full throttle) of 432mph at 25,500ft in FS gear (Full

Supercharger, providing plus 18lb/sq in boost pressure). The service ceiling was 40,100ft and the rate of climb was 2,480ft per minute at 12lb/sq in boost. For the Merlin XX version the maximum speed at sea level was 331mph in MS gear and the maximum speed at full throttle height was 393mph at 18,600ft in FS gear (plus 12lb/sq in boost pressure); service ceiling was 36,300ft and rate of climb 2,360ft per minute at 9lb/sq in boost.

The first Mustang to be earmarked for conversion was AG518, but, as previously mentioned, this one was grounded, being succeeded by AM121 which arrived at Hucknall on 7 June 1942 but was, in fact, the last to be converted, being flown on performance calibration and investigation for eight months. Design work on the Merlin 61 installation went ahead with the aid of AG518, and it was hoped to have the Merlin 65 or 66 ready in time for the first flight; these newer variants differed from the Mk 61 in having different supercharger gear ratios to enable maximum power to be attained at a lower altitude, and Bendix Stromberg fuel injectors in place of the float or RAE Anti-G type carburettors, the former having the advantage of not cutting out under high-G conditions. The Merlin 65 gave 1,705bhp at 5,750ft compared to the Merlin 61's 1,565bhp at 12,000ft; the former was designated RM10SM and the latter RM8SM under the Rolls-Royce system. The five Mustangs converted were to be known officially as Mustang Xs, although at Hucknall they were always called just Merlin Mustangs. They were delivered to Hucknall from the Lockheed Aircraft Corporation's handling units for American aircraft at Speke Airport, Liverpool, and Abbotsinch, in June and August 1942, and at first three aircraft, AM121, AL963 and AL975, all delivered in June, were intended for conversion, with AM203 and AM208 joining the conversion programme in August at the request of the USAAF in the United Kingdom, who wanted to evaluate the Merlin Mustang for themselves before production deliveries in the States could be expected to start. In the end both these two remained in British hands, although the Americans did evaluate AM121.

As an insurance against the possibility, admittedly not very serious, that the Americans might not approve the Merlin-powered Mustang for production in the States, Rolls-Royce prepared the outlines of a scheme for the conversion of up to 500 of the RAF's Allison-engined Mustang Is to Merlin power; this job, had it been approved, could have been undertaken either by Rolls-Royce itself or by some other manufacturer under Air Ministry contract. Rolls already had experience of similar conversions, replacing the Merlin IIs or IIIs of Hurricane Is from 1940 with Merlin XXs to bring them to Hurricane II standard, and in the spring of 1942 had begun converting over 300 Spitfire Vs to Mk IX standard by replacing their Merlin 45s with Merlin 61s. Conversions such as these had been simplified by the development of the 'power egg' concept, in which the engine, its mounting, its associated plumbing and the cowling were supplied as a complete unit ready for bolting on to the firewall. In the event the proposed conversion of Allison-engined Mustang Is was rendered unnecessary by US acceptance of the Merlin Mustang and the conversion of two aircraft, initially known as XP–78s, in the States to take the 1,520hp Packard-built Merlin V–1650–3, equivalent to the Merlin 61; these were later redesignated XP–51Bs.

Meanwhile design work was continuing on the installation of the Merlin 61 which, although it could be accommodated within the existing cowling shape with little modification, needed a modified mounting structure because the width across the supercharger casing at the rear of the engine was greater than the distance between the existing engine mounting pick-up points on the firewall. An intermediate mounting structure was introduced between the firewall pick-up points and the rear of the engine at the blower casing, and from the lower points of this structure projected the two Rolls-Royce 'Consus' or Convergent Suspension mounting members which incorporated rubber-sprung pick-ups on to which the engine was bolted. Externally, the most obvious difference was moving the carburettor air intake from above the nose, where it was for the Allison V–1710's down-draught carburettor, to below the nose to cater for the Merlin's up-draught induction system, and on the Mustang Xs this intake scoop was of varying shape, and deeper than on the P–51B and later production Merlin variants. Originally it was proposed to retain the above-cowling intake for serving the intercooler radiator; the intercooler's function was to lower the temperature of the fuel vapour charge which, by the time it had been compressed twice in the two supercharger stages, would have risen to a temperature very close to that of combustion, and—without the intercooler—would very probably have detonated as it entered the cylinders. By lowering the temperature of the charge in this way, the intercooler increased its density, which made possible increased power for a given boost pressure. The intercooler was cooled by a small separate radiator, suspended in the Mustang X under the forward part of the engine, and this radiator's air exit louvres were sited further aft in the cowling panel ahead of the main firewall.

One result of moving the carburettor intake from above the cowling to underneath was that the pilot's sight line along the top of the cowling was improved by an extra $1\frac{1}{2}$ degrees, and it was also realised that by raising the engine thrust line slightly the bulkiness of the lower cowling could be reduced; so the engine itself was elevated by $3\frac{1}{2}$in. This also made it possible to reduce the size of the carburettor intake trunking and the associated intake elbow. At first a pressurised fuel system was proposed in place of the existing electrically driven fuel booster pump, but instead an alternative was chosen—an immersed fuel pump in each wing tank. This enabled the fuel cooler to be deleted from its position within the intercooler radiator, although this was not in fact done for the initial Mustang X flights. To accommodate the immersed pumps, the collapsible-type Mareng fuel tanks were replaced by two tinned steel tanks, while the hydraulic system was modified to provide for automatic radiator flap operation and supercharger speed control. Two types of Rotol propeller were to be evaluated in flight trials, an 11ft 4in diameter four-blader specially designed for the Mustang X with a reduction gear ratio of 0·42 to 1, and a standard Spitfire IX 10ft 9in diameter airscrew with four Jablo Hydulignum blades, and a reduction gear ratio of 0·477 to 1.

The first conversion flies
By early October 1942 the first Mustang X conversion, AL975/G, was completed and, after ground running, made a thirty-minute maiden flight on the 13th of that month piloted by Rolls-Royce's Chief Test Pilot, Captain R. T. Shepherd, with a Merlin 65 driving the 10ft 9in diameter propeller. (Contrary to what has so often been stated, the Merlin 61 did not fly in any of the Mustang Xs, all of which initially had Merlin 65s that had been—except for two engines—modified from Mk 61s; the Mk 65s were all experimental engines, and that fitted to AL975/G had previously been installed, as a Mk 61, in a Spitfire IX.) With the Merlin 65, the estimated maximum speed in FS gear was 427mph at 21,000ft and in MS gear 392mph at 9,600ft. The initial flights were made with Mareng fuel tanks as the tinned steel ones were not yet ready, and during the first flight, in which a speed of 376mph was achieved, a pressure build-up within the cowling caused it to become loose. There then followed some experiment to see if an improvement in speed could be gained by modifying the intercooler radiator air exit louvres and the main radiator ducting; at the moment there was a shortfall of some 16mph below the estimated figure with these radiator configurations. All but 2mph of this was recovered by reducing the exit area of the main radiator duct by almost a half; also tried were changing the reduction gear ratio to 0·42 to 1 with the same Spitfire IX propeller, streamlining the intercooler radiator air exit louvres, fitting a larger intercooler radiator and deleting the fuel cooler, and flattening the bottom section of the cowling slightly. The result was a small speed recovery and an improvement in the intercooler's effectiveness.

For the seventh flight the 11ft 4in diameter propeller was fitted, and the intercooler radiator exit louvres on the starboard side were blanked off, but there was no improvement in speed, and there was even a small drop on the next flight with all the louvres open. It was thought that one reason for the speed shortfall might be that air passing through the intercooler radiator into the engine bay was being ejected through the cowling joints at right-angles to the flight path, and to overcome this a duct was fitted allowing the air to be piped directly from the radiator overboard, thus dispensing with the need for the louvres, which were then blanked off. For the ninth flight a tinned steel tank replaced the Mareng tank in the port wing, which now made it possible to obtain performance figures in both MS and FS gears instead of MS gear only as before, and on 8 November a flight revealed a speed of 413mph in FS gear, or 14mph short of the estimate, and 390mph in MS gear.

But surprisingly when the original 10ft 9in diameter propeller was refitted, the speed in FS gear increased by 9mph to 422mph, and flight tests confirmed that performance figures for this prop were contrary to expectation, being low below 26,000ft and high above this altitude. On the early flights there was also some trouble with the undercarriage doors opening in flight, but this was largely cured by re-adjusting the undercarriage wheel flap lock. For the next test flights the intercooler radiator louvres were unblanked, and it was found that the duct recently fitted was not, in fact, responsible for the 9mph speed increase that occurred when the original prop was refitted. Although there was still

This front view of the second Mustang X conversion, AM208, emphasises how much larger the nose intake was than on production P–51Bs (*RR*)

a speed shortfall, the rate of climb with the Merlin 65 proved to be better at low altitudes than the estimates, and practically the same from 13,000ft to 34,000ft. After the existing engine had suffered a bearing failure, it was removed and replaced by another Merlin 65, and with this the design speed of 427mph was eventually attained after the main radiator front flap was fixed in a permanent position and sealed.

In February 1943 AL975/G was fitted with an RM11SM Merlin 70 engine, which had a maximum power output 50bhp less than the Merlin 65's, the same supercharger gear ratios as the Merlin 61 and a reduction gear ratio of 0·477 to 1. Another change made, following flight trials with Mustang X AM208, was the addition of a dorsal fillet to the fin to improve directional stability; a large change in directional trim at high power and speeds had been experienced and there was a tendency to sideslip easily during manoeuvres; the dorsal fillet fitted to AL975/G but not, surprisingly, to AM208 gave only a marginal improvement and so the fin chord on AL975/G was increased to give an extra 3sq ft of area, and this did the trick. Production Merlin Mustangs were not quite as pleasant to fly as the Allison versions, partly because of this directional instability and the extra torque generated by the higher-powered engine. A good deal of flying was carried out over the next year

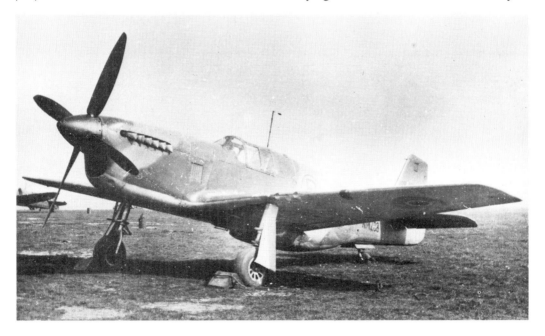

or so with the development of a new system of cooling, known as shunt cooling, in the Merlin 70; this was used in the Messerschmitt Bf 109E, a captured example of which had been evaluated by Rolls-Royce, and shunt cooling offered a number of advantages over the existing method, namely, greater efficiency, weight saving, simplification in piping and ducting, a higher coolant flow rate combined with a decrease in pressure, and the absence of cavitation, or the formation of bubbles in the coolant. The greater efficiency meant that less coolant capacity was needed and hence a smaller header tank, that on AL975/G being reduced in weight from 18lb to 4lb. Shunt cooling was later used in the de Havilland DH 103 Hornet fighter then in the design stage, and this method was also tested on the Merlin 71 Special fitted to AL975 (now without the '/G' suffix) in May 1944; the Mk 71 was the same as the Mk 70 but with a cabin blower fitted. AL975's career ended when it suffered an engine failure and was badly damaged in the resulting wheels-up landing at Fradswell in Staffordshire on 14 March 1945.

Second and later conversions
The second Mustang X conversion was AM208, which made its first flight on 13 November 1942 flown, like the first, by Captain R. T. Shepherd and fitted with a Merlin 65 driving a 10ft 9in diameter propeller. It had the main radiator front flap permanently fixed and sealed; this modification had originally been applied on an Allison-engined Mustang which had shown a speed increase of 6–7mph as a result, and it was applied to AL975/G after much of the work in getting the intercooler radiator and main radiator exit configurations right had been done. It was this mod that finally made it possible for the Merlin 65-powered Mustang to exceed its estimated top speed of 427mph at 21,000ft in FS gear, so vindicating the whole idea of fitting the Merlin; performance trials with AM208 at the Aircraft and Armament Experimental Establishment at Boscombe Down, where it had been delivered on 28 November, culminated in April 1943 with maximum true air speeds of 406mph at 10,000ft in MS gear and 433 mph at 22,000ft in FS gear at the combat

rating of 18lb/sq in boost. The radiator front flap modification had resulted in a top speed increase of 11mph over AL975/G without this feature; AM208 and the three subsequent conversions did not feature the slight bulge in the lower engine cowling that AL975/G had in its original form. After the speed tests another Merlin 65 was fitted to AM208 in place of its original powerplant, and climb trials were undertaken; these showed a rate of climb of 3,560ft per minute at 7,500ft in MS gear and 2,840ft per minute at 19,000ft in FS gear, the time to reach 20,000ft being 6·3 minutes.

The third conversion was AM203, first flown on 13 December 1942, again by Captain Shepherd, and also fitted with a Merlin 65, this time with the 11ft 4in diameter propeller. AM203 was sprayed in a high gloss finish by Sanderson & Holmes, the Derby firm of coachbuilders, to evaluate the effect of such a finish on performance compared with the standard matt surface camouflage scheme. After preliminary trials at Hucknall and Boscombe Down, AM203 went to the Air Fighting Development Unit at Duxford on 23 December, and here achieved a maximum level speed of 431mph at the full throttle height of 21,800ft. When the 10ft 9in diameter propeller was fitted, the same thing happened as on AL975/G—an unexpected increase, this time by only 3mph in FS gear, of maximum speed. It might be thought that the smaller airscrew, being lighter and offering slightly less drag, would naturally produce a higher speed, but in fact more engine power was needed to overcome the difference in blade area between the two propellers, or, for the same power setting, a slight decrease in speed might be expected. The original 11ft 4in prop was refitted to AM203 and, after returning to the AFDU at Duxford late in January, it was loaned to the USAAF for a few weeks, being the first Merlin Mustang to be evaluated by them. It returned to Hucknall on 22 March for respraying in matt surface camouflage for performance trials to compare with the previous high gloss finish; at the same time a dorsal fin was fitted. But surprisingly there was found to be no difference at all in speed between the two finishes, and this was put down to the Mustang's very smooth construction with flush riveting and no airflow-interrupting discontinuities at the skin joints. After going back to the AFDU on 5 May it returned to Hucknall in late October but was not used for any further engine development. In February 1944 AM203 was turned over to No 12 Group Communications Flight, which was also based at Hucknall, and ended its career with this unit when it made a forced landing in December and was written off.

The fourth conversion, AL963, first flew with a Merlin 65 on 21 January 1943 in the hands of Captain Shepherd, going to the AFDU at Duxford a week later for Service trials, returning to Hucknall early in February for the fitting of a dorsal fin. After spending another fortnight at Duxford it then returned to Hucknall in late February. It was re-engined with a Merlin 65 Special with an SU Mk 2 fuel injector pump in place of the previous Bendix-Stromberg fuel injector; the former was chosen as the most convenient method of producing the fuel metering characteristics necessitated by the increased fuel flow. The new engine's compression ratio was reduced from 6:1 to 5:1 with 100 octane fuel, and the maximum permissible boost pressure was increased to 23lb/sq in to give a still better low-altitude performance. The Merlin 65 Special with these features was intended to provide

The third Mustang X conversion, AM203, was sprayed in a high gloss finish which, surprisingly, gave no advantage in speed over the standard matt surface camouflage (*RR*)

preliminary data for the coming RM14SM Merlin 100 series which featured a super-charger of greater capacity giving higher full throttle heights, and a maximum boost pressure of 25lb/sq in. The higher-boosted Merlin 65 Special at full boost gave AL963 a maximum speed of 370mph at 1,000ft, or 17mph faster than with the Merlin 65, and 424mph at 21,000ft in FS gear, or 12mph faster at the same height than with the Merlin 65; at 25,000ft both the Merlin 65 and the Special gave a speed of 420mph. Rates of climb also improved with the 65 Special by 900ft per minute from 3,800 to 4,700ft per minute from ground level up to 3,600ft, and by 940ft per minute from 3,040 to 3,980ft per minute at 15,200ft.

After doing $45\frac{3}{4}$ hours flying time in AL963 the Merlin 65 Special was replaced by a Merlin 66 for evaluating a new type of intercooler. This was relocated from its position beneath the nose and mounted in series with the main radiator just aft of the wings, and it had an integral header tank containing the coolant instead of a separately mounted tank as before. This resiting made it possible to reduce appreciably the size of the nose intake to something approximating that of the production P–51B. But the main radiator's efficiency was impaired by having the intercooler radiator mounted directly in front of it and screening a certain area of it. After a few hours flying, AL963 therefore reverted to the original radiator configuration as Rolls-Royce had now agreed to the

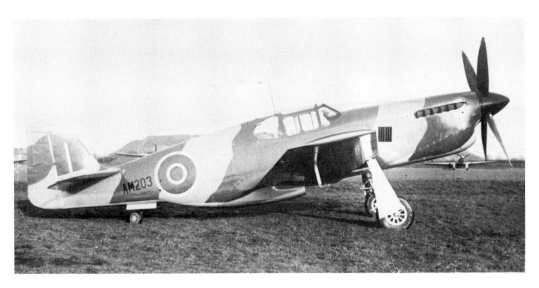

American design for the production P–51B of a larger matrix incorporating both radiators and requiring a slightly deeper ventral intake to accommodate it. The Merlin 66 was removed and replaced by the previously fitted Mk 65 Special, with which reliability tests of the SU fuel injector pump were now undertaken. At some time prior to the Merlin 66 intercooler tests the dorsal fin of AL963 had been removed and replaced by the leading edge fin extension also applied to AL975/G. AL963 completed 102½ hours of Merlin development up to 6 January 1944, when it was stored, and eventually struck off charge on 23 November that year.

The fifth Mustang X conversion to fly, AM121, was, as mentioned earlier, the first to arrive at Hucknall for conversion but instead was kept flying on performance calibration for eight months. It made its first flight on 7 February 1943 in the hands of Captain R. T. Shepherd with the Merlin 65 that had been originally installed in AL975/G. By this time most of the development flying had been completed, and AM121 was earmarked for evaluation by the USAAF; it went to the AFDU at Duxford at the end of February for Service trials and they loaned it to the US Eighth Air Force Fighter Command at Bovingdon for trials. It was returned to Hucknall on 3 May for the fitting of the broader chord fin similar to that of AL975/G, and on 11 May it went to the Rotol Flight Test Department at Staverton for a spell of intensive test flying of the 0·020in thick Rotoloid protective coating for the propeller blades under normal conditions and in all weathers. Between 13 and 27 May a total of 150 hours were flown, or over 10 hours a day —remarkable for a fighter, and equal to the best airliner utilisation figures of post-war years, as well as proving the reliability of the Merlin 65 installation. This intensive flying showed that large areas of the Rotoloid coating had been shed from the blades as in its present form it was too thin; further development of a 0·030in thick coating was then pursued. AM121 returned to Hucknall on 17 June, where it was re-engined with another Merlin 65, and on the 26th it went to the Eighth Air Force Fighter Command's Air Technical Section at Bovingdon. While in USAAF service it was coloured olive-drab all over, with white

chordwise stripes on the inner wings and tailplane and across the fin and rudder, and the USAAF 'star and bars' insignia replaced the RAF roundels and fin flash. The code letters R–VQ were applied in white, and the RAF serial in the same colour appeared just below the fin stripe; the airscrew spinner and front of the cowling were also painted white. AM121 was finally broken down for spares in August 1944.

In addition to the development work on the Merlin installation, Rolls-Royce did a project study of a Griffon 61-engined version of the Mustang. This was unusual in that the engine was located aft of the cockpit and drove a contra-rotating airscrew via an extension shaft, as in the Bell P–39 Airacobra. But the Airacobra had suffered a number of teething troubles as a result of its buried engine installation, and most of the 675 ordered by the RAF had been diverted to the Soviet Union or the USAAF; nearly 10,000 were built altogether. The buried engine layout had the disadvantage that a major redesign was necessary if a later and slightly longer version of the original engine was to be fitted during the course of development. The Griffon 61 Mustang was not built, although Mustang 1 AM148 was earmarked for a Griffon installation, but a mock-up was made, and among the changes made necessary by the engine position was that the cockpit was moved further forward. When a Griffon 57 finally powered a Mustang in 1975, namely the P–51D N7715C raced by Roy McClain and sponsored by Red Baron Flying Services of Idaho Falls, it was installed in the conventional position, driving a modified de Havilland six-blade contra-rotating airscrew.

The Merlin Mustang goes into service
While Rolls-Royce was engaged in development flying of the Mustang Xs during the winter of 1942–3 their flight test data were forwarded to North American to form the basis of the production Merlin Mustang, the P–51B. This was a complete redesign, powered by a 1,520hp Packard-built Merlin V–1650–3 with two-stage, two-speed supercharger and intercooler, corresponding to the Merlin 61. Two Mustang IAs originally destined for the RAF were converted to have this engine, being redesignated XP–78 at first, this being changed after a short while

The XP–78, soon redesignated XP–51B, in its original form with guns removed and a different carburettor air intake to that of production P–51Bs (*RIC*)

Another view of one of the two cannon-armed Mustang IAs destined for the RAF that were converted to have Packard Merlin V–1650–3s as XP–51Bs. This view shows the boundary layer splitter gap between the ventral radiator scoop and the fuselage (*RR*)

to XP–51B. Before these two prototypes had even flown, General 'Hap' Arnold was able to tell President Roosevelt in November 1942 that approximately 2,200 P–51Bs had been ordered for the USAAF; the first production Bs were delivered in June 1943. A second production line at North American's Dallas, Texas plant was opened, the Dallas-built variant, the P–51C, otherwise the

same as the P–51B, beginning to come off the line in August 1943. Altogether 1,988 P–51Bs and 1,750 P–51Cs were built for the USAAF.

The prototype XP–51Bs, the first of which flew on 30 November 1942, had airframes strengthened for the higher power and new ailerons were fitted. The nose-mounted intercooler radiator of the Mustang Xs was now replaced by a larger radiator matrix incorporating both main and intercooler radiators, and served by a deeper ventral air scoop; this enabled the rather bulbous nose intake of the Mustang Xs to be replaced by one of much smaller diameter housing only the carburettor air intake and its trunking, the intake being made integral with the engine mount front frame assembly. Instead of the Mustang X's Rotol airscrews of 10ft 9in or 11ft 4in diameter and pointed blades, the XP–51Bs and P–51Bs had four-blade Hamilton Standard Hydromatic automatic constant-speed airscrews of 11ft 2in diameter with 'paddle' blades much less finely pointed than those of the Mustang X. The XP–51Bs also had stronger underwing racks to take two 1,000lb bombs or their equivalent weight in fuel in the shape of two 75 or 150 us gal drop tanks.

The XP–51Bs had a gross weight of 8,430lb and a maximum speed of 441mph, or 51mph faster than the Allison-engined P–51A. The production P–51B–15–NA with the Packard Merlin V–1650–7 corresponding to the Merlin 68 had a quoted maximum speed of 437mph at 30,000ft, but a North American flight test report of January 1944 for the P–51B–1–NA at a test weight of 8,460lb revealed a maximum speed of 453mph TAS at 28,800ft at 67in of mercury (Hg) boost and 1,298hp war emergency power in FS gear and critical altitude. The maximum rate of climb under war emergency power was 3,900ft per minute at 12,800ft, the time to 20,000ft at the same power rating was 5·5 minutes, and the service ceiling was 44,200ft. This top speed seems to suggest that the USAAF's and manufacturer's figures tended to err on the side of caution when quoting maximum performance; it was only 16mph short of the world air speed record set up on 26 April 1939 by the Messerschmitt Bf 109R, which in reality was not a special version of the well-known Bf 109, as the Germans claimed, but a completely new design, the Me 209V1.

The production P–51B differed very little from the XP–51Bs, and had four or six 0·5in Browning MG 53 machine-guns in the wings, with a total of 1,260 rounds. The point of convergence with all six guns firing was adjustable from 150 to 400yd, with 250yd being the standard figure. Each 0·5in calibre Browning weighed 64lb and could be replaced in a few minutes, the gun bays being easily accessible through servicing panels in the upper wing surface.

The first USAAF unit to fly the Merlin Mustang was the 354th Fighter Group which, having trained and worked up in the States on Bell P–39 Airacobras, had left these behind and sailed for England on 20 October 1943 to join the new 9th Air Force, at first being based temporarily at Greenham Common in Berkshire. It was here on 11 November that the Group received its first P–51B–1–NAs, and two days later the unit moved to its first combat base at Boxted in Essex. At that time USAAF heavy bomber units were suffering a loss rate of some 10 per cent in their daylight raids over Germany, and two deep penetration raids in particular on 17 August, on the ball-bearing works at Schweinfurt and the Messerschmitt plant at Regensburg, had suffered heavy casualties. The Mustang's capabilities as a long-range escort fighter were badly needed by the hard-pressed B–17 Fortress groups, as witness these vivid extracts from an account of the Regensburg mission by the co-pilot of a B–17 of the last Group in the formation, which was hit harder than any other:

On we flew through the strewn wake of a desperate air battle, where disintegrating aircraft were commonplace and sixty chutes in the air at one time were hardly worth a second look . . .

Ten minutes, twenty minutes, thirty minutes, and still no let-up in the attacks. The fighters queued up like a bread line and let us have it. Each second of time had a cannon shell in it . . .

After we had been under constant attack for a solid hour, it appeared certain that our Group was faced with annihilation. Seven of us had been shot down, the sky was still mottled with

P–51B Mustangs of the 354th Fighter Group, US 8th Air Force, which was the first USAAF unit to fly the Merlin Mustang; these two belong to the 355th Fighter Sqn of that Group at Boxted, Essex (*USO*)

rising fighters, and it was only 11.20 hours, with target time still 35 minutes away. I doubt if a man in the Group visualised the possibility of our getting much further without one hundred per cent loss. I know that I had long since mentally accepted the fact of death, and that it was simply a question of the next second or the next minute. I learned first-hand that a man can resign himself to the certainty of death without becoming panicky. Our Group fire power was reduced 33 per cent; ammunition was running low. Our tail guns had to be replenished from another gun station. Gunners were becoming exhausted . . .

After bombing the target successfully, the writer concludes:

At 18.15 hours, with red lights showing on all the fuel tanks in my ship, the seven B–17s of the Group which were still in formation circled over a North African aerodrome and landed. Our crew was unscratched . . . We slept on the hard ground under the wings of our B–17, but the good earth felt softer than a silk pillow.

But the Mustang's arrival was to change dramatically this nightmare picture of a long unescorted bombing trip across Europe; its ability to escort the bombers all the way to their targets and still meet German fighters on equal terms after jettisoning nearly empty drop tanks put a severe tactical strain on the German defences and, by cutting losses, added greatly to the effectiveness of the US daylight bombing offensive. The effect the Mustangs had on the bomber crews' morale can well be imagined, and many crippled bombers owed their return to the presence of escorting P–51s. Meanwhile, the 354th Fighter Group flew their first mission with the P–51Bs, a sweep over Belgium and the Pas de Calais, on 1 December, twenty-three Mustangs being led by the CO, Lt-Colonel Don Blakeslee, a veteran of the American Eagle squadron. Bomber escort began on the 5th under the operational control of the 8th Air Force, and on the fifth mission, to Bremen, on the 16th the first P–51B 'kill' was scored by Lt Charles F. Gumm of the 355th Squadron who brought down a Bf 110; three more claims by other pilots followed on the 20th. The first long-range escort mission had been flown on the 13th to Kiel, a distance of 490 miles each way; this was a record at the time.

But those early missions had also shown up a number of problems only to be expected with a new version of an aircraft operating at higher altitudes than before. The windscreen heating was insufficient at height, with some frosting over liable to occur; coolant leaks occurred, causing engines to overheat; spark plugs fouled up quickly because of the retarded engine setting necessary for long-range escort flights,

with their need to save fuel; and there was
persistent jamming of the guns in tight
turns until modifications were made to the
ammunition belts. By the end of 1943 the
354th Group had destroyed only eight
enemy aircraft and had lost eight pilots,
but things began to improve in the New
Year. Over Kiel on 5 January 1944 the
P–51Bs tangled with Messerschmitt Bf 110s
and Focke-Wulf Fw 190s, destroying
eighteen German fighters without loss.

On the 11th the P–51Bs escorted B–17
Fortresses on a raid on Oschersleben and
the German fighters showed up in force,
resulting in a number of desperate battles.
In the course of these a lone Mustang found
itself the sole defender of a Fortress group
that was being attacked by some three dozen
German fighters and the B–17 crews
watched amazed as the P–51B, with all its
four guns blazing, twice attacked the enemy
fighters. With only two guns firing, it
returned for a third time to break up the
German attack and then, by now with only
one gun functioning properly, it came back
twice more at the enemy aircraft. Major
James H. Howard, the pilot, shot down
three Germans in thirty minutes as the sole
protector of the bomber group, and probably destroyed another three; the B–17
crews claimed he got at least six. It was
their witness of his great gallantry that led
to the award of the coveted Congressional
Medal of Honour to Major Howard, one of
the few occasions when it went to a fighter
pilot. Howard, promoted to Lt-Colonel, took
over as Group CO on 12 February after the
loss of Colonel Kenneth R. Martin the previous day in a collision over Frankfurt with
a German aircraft; Martin managed to bail
out and survived as a POW.

From late March the Group began to fly
more and more tactical support missions,
beginning with a dive-bombing attack on the
Creil marshalling yards in France with
500lb bombs on 26 March. On 10 April, for
the first time, two missions were flown in a
day, dive bombing in the morning and
escorting Martin B–26 Marauders in the
afternoon; Lt-Colonel G. R. Bickell had just
replaced Colonel Howard as the CO that day.
A week later the Group moved to Lashen-
don in Kent in preparation for D-Day and
it was here that the 354th received its first
Distinguished Unit Citation for introducing
the Merlin Mustang into service and for the
excellent bomber escort it had provided
from December 1943 to 15 May 1944. Until
February that year, when new P–51B units

began to be formed, the 354th and its three constituent Squadrons, the 353rd, the 355th and the 356th, had been the sole operational group with the Merlin Mustang.

The second P–51B group was the 357th, based at Leiston in Suffolk, which made its operational debut in February 1944, and the third P–51B group was the 363rd at Rivenhall in Essex, which became operational on 22 February. Both these groups were under the 9th Air Force initially, although the 357th very soon transferred to the 8th Air Force. The 4th Fighter Group at Debden in Essex had also converted to P–51Bs from P–47 Thunderbolts by 25 February that year, and went on to destroy 1,000 enemy aircraft by the end of the war. It was on 3 March that P–51Bs for the first time escorted B–17 Fortresses and B–24 Liberators all the way on the 1,100-mile round trip to Berlin, an event that was to lead Reichsmarschall Herman Goering to comment later: 'the day that I saw American fighters over Berlin was the day that I realised that Germany would lose the war'.

The 354th Group flew many tactical support missions after D-Day, and also found time for a spot of V–1 hunting, as its base was in the path of the flying bombs launched from France. On one night late in June several pilots of the 355th Squadron went up and Lt Joe Powers brought down $2\frac{1}{2}$ V–1s in a sortie of $4\frac{1}{2}$ hours. By the end of the month the Group had crossed to France, being based ten miles behind the front line at A–2 airfield, Criqueville, and it was here that an unusual request was received—to fly the Supreme Allied Commander, General Eisenhower, over the Normandy battlefields in one of the Group's Mustangs. A P–51B–5–NA, 43–6877, was specially modified in the United Kingdom by the Group, a second seat being installed aft of the pilot's and the radio and other equipment normally occupying this area being re-located. This Mustang, an old one that had been taken off operations, is often mistakenly referred to as a TP–51D; its only apparent difference from other P–51Bs was an enlarged window panel for the passenger to look out of. It flew General Eisenhower for the first time early in July, and was subsequently used for communications, carrying two people on several other occasions. Several more P–51Bs and Cs were later

converted to two-seaters at field bases during 1944–5. The 354th continued to do ground support missions from Criqueville and moved up to the A–31 landing ground at Gael on 13 August. Twelve days later the Group carried out six fighter sweeps in which fifty-one enemy aircraft were destroyed—an achievement which won the Group its second Distinguished Unit Citation. In November the 354th, much against its will, re-equipped with the Republic P–47D Thunderbolt but, by protesting pretty forcefully through the appropriate channels, eventually got back on to Mustangs, re-equipping with P–51Ds in February 1945.

Meanwhile, as P–51B production built up, some modifications were incorporated in the light of operational experience. The last 550 Bs to be built became P–51B–7–NA to P–51B–10–NA variants with the addition of a self-sealing 85 US gal fuel tank in the fuselage behind the pilot, bringing total internal fuel capacity to 269 US gal; some earlier P–51Bs and Cs were also fitted in the field with this fuselage fuel tank. The P–51B–15–NA had as powerplant the 1,450hp Packard Merlin V–1650–7, corresponding to the Merlin 68 of British production and with a higher war emergency rating of 1,695hp at 10,300ft. Some P–51Bs and Cs were also fitted in Britain with the bulged, sliding Malcolm cockpit hood of the Mustang III. The original sideways-hingeing cockpit canopy had only limited rear view, and so this frameless hood, similar to that of the Spitfire and designed by R. Malcolm, was first fitted to a Mk III at Boscombe Down. It was successful enough to be fitted to most Mustang IIIs after they had arrived in England for the RAF, and it also increased the headroom, the lack of which had been a cause of complaint by the pilots of the RAF's No 65 Squadron. But the Malcolm canopy, although successful, was seen as a temporary measure and both the USAAF and RAF were still concerned about the rear view. This led to the P–51D, in which a large moulded plastic 'bubble'-type sliding canopy was combined with a cut-down rear fuselage which greatly improved rear vision, and this canopy was tested on P–51B–1–NA 43–12102, which also had the redesigned rear fuselage.

Apart from the Malcolm canopy, another

important British development which helped to make the Mustang such an outstanding long-range escort was the 108 US gal drop tank made of plastic and compressed paper held together by glue. When the first Mustang X began to show the increase in performance the Merlin had made possible, the need became evident for a larger drop tank than the 75 US gal aluminium one for long-range escort flights to Berlin or beyond, and the US 8th Air Force asked one of the American base depots in England to design such a tank. This task was taken up by two British engineers, André Rousseau and Thomas B. O'Reilly, who were joined by A. A. Richards, chief engineer of a British firm which designed drop tanks, while on the American side Lt-Colonel Cass Hough and Lt Schafer of the 8th Air Force also took a hand. A 108 US gal tank was designed in a short time but it was soon obvious that there would be insufficient aluminium supplies in Britain to meet the demand, and shipping it from the States would pose many problems. So the use of much-needed aluminium for an expendable item was abandoned in favour of the plastic/pressed paper substitute; both Britain and America

A Mustang III of the Balkan Air Force being fitted with 100gal drop tanks. The three discs beneath the wing in line and inboard of the wing tip are coloured recognition lights (*IWM*)

had experimented with paper as a possible fuel tank material as far back as 1936.

Fuel could not be stored in these tanks as it would cause the paper and glue to come apart after a day or two, but this did not matter, as the tanks were fueled up before take-off and jettisoned four hours or more later. They could be used as effective incendiary bombs, being jettisoned over a target in a skip bombing run and then the Mustang pilot would ignite the fuel with his machine-guns. These plastic/paper tanks proved successful enough to warrant a demand for no less than 24,000 of them a month, and to meet this need, two British firms with the aid of 45 small subcontractors employing 20–100 people each, many of them women, went into production. Ironically enough, after 50,000 had been used in combat the US War Department sent a memo to the 8th Air Force stating that the idea was unworkable and that these tanks should not be procured.

P–51B Mustangs, soon followed by

Four P–51Bs of the 325th Fighter Group, us 15th Air Force, escort B–17G Fortresses in a shuttle bombing raid over Germany from Mediterranean bases on into Russia (*USO*)

P–51Cs, began operating with the us 15th Air Force in Italy from early in 1944, and they served here alongside RAF Mustang IIIs. On 5 May 1944 Mustangs of the Desert Air Force achieved a notable piece of dambusting when, accompanied by Curtiss Kittyhawks and operating from bases in eastern Italy, they attacked and breached the great Pescara dam by bombing, without suffering any losses. This raid had been ordered by General Alexander, the C-in-C Allied Armies in Italy, as a prelude to his offensive aimed at destroying German forces south of Rome, and the floods from the broken dam gave so much protection to the right wing of the 8th Army that it became possible to move troops from that flank to reinforce the Fifth Army under General Mark Clark on the left of the Allied line, between the Mediterranean and the River Liri.

By April 1944 P–51B Mustangs were equipping the 311th Group of the us 10th Air Force based in India near the Burmese border, and were flying sorties in support of airborne troops attacking Japanese lines of communication some 200 miles behind the front in northern Burma. At the same time other P–51Bs began to equip units of the us 14th Air Force in China itself, where supplies of every kind had to be flown in over the southern spurs of the Himalayas known as 'the Hump'. The China-based P 51Bs did not, for this reason, enjoy quite the same level of logistic support that their counterparts in Europe did, and some interesting in-the-field modifications were evolved for the carriage of external 'stores'. These included the carriage of two 250lb bombs on racks just outboard of the two 75 us gal underwing drop tanks; a cluster of three 100lb bombs under each wing bomb rack, plus a second cluster of eighteen anti-personnel fragmentation bombs under a second, strut-braced pylon just outboard of each wing rack; three 100lb HE bombs under each of these secondary pylons with a 75 us gal drop tank inboard; and four 75 us gal tanks under the wings, the two extra ones likewise under the strut-braced outboard pylons. These, together with the 85 gal fuselage fuel tank, gave a total tankage

A P–51C–5–NT 42–103433: H–5M being serviced
on a captured airfield with the tail of a Ju 188 to
the right; note the Malcolm hood fitted (*USO*)

Mustang IIIs of No 19 Sqn, first RAF unit to
equip with this mark; these are fitted with the
bulged, sliding Malcolm cockpit canopies (*IWM*)

of no less than 569 US gallons and a resulting range of 2,700 miles. As related in Chapter 5, ex-USAAF P–51Bs were later acquired for the Chinese Nationalist Air Force.

The P–51C–NT Mustang was built at the new Dallas, Texas plant but was otherwise the same as the P–51B, with the same Packard Merlin V–1650–3 engine and four or six 0·5in Browning MG 53 machineguns; altogether 1,750 of all P–51C subvariants (Blocks 1–11) were built. Some were fitted in the field with the 85 US gal fuselage fuel tank and some were also fitted in Britain with the bulged, sliding Malcolm cockpit canopy. The P–51C–5–NT to P–51C–10–NT variants had the Packard Merlin V–1650–7 engine with the higher war emergency rating of 1,695hp at 10,300ft.

The F–6C was a tactical reconnaissance version of the P–51B and P–51C, a total of seventy-one F–6C–NAs being converted from P–51B–NAs and twenty F–6C–NTs converted from P–51C–NTs; they had one K–17, one K–22 or two K–24 cameras in the rear fuselage and carried full armament. Powerplant was the Packard Merlin V–1650–7, which gave a maximum speed of 430mph, and gross weight was 10,000lb. Some F–6Cs were later fitted in Britain with the Malcolm cockpit canopy.

The Mustang III

The RAF version of the P–51B and P–51C was the Mustang III, which was supplied under Lend-Lease with the original sideways hingeing cockpit canopy, but, as related earlier, most Mk IIIs were retrofitted after delivery with the Malcolm bulged canopy. Altogether 910 Mustang IIIs were delivered, of which 274 corresponded to the P–51B (serials FB100–FB124, FX848–FX999, FZ100–FZ147, FZ149–FZ197 and FR411) while the remaining 636 (serials FB125–FB399, HB821–HB961 and KH421–KH640) were equivalent to the P–51C. Three Mustangs were also taken over in the Middle East from the USAAF and given the serials HK944–HK946, while almost at the end of the war a batch of thirty-five USAAF P–51Bs and P–51Cs taken over became SR406–SR440. Mustang III FX893 was tested at

Boscombe Down with four rocket projectiles in two tiers of two under each wing. Mustang IIIs first entered service with No 19 Squadron at Ford, Sussex, in February 1944 and were used as bomber escorts and later as fighter-bombers with the 2nd Tactical Air Force operating from French bases. At the end of 1944 Mustangs were removed from the 2nd TAF's control and rejoined Fighter Command's strength in the United Kingdom, while other Mustang squadrons had been in action against the V–1 flying bombs, destroying a total of 232 of them by 5 September 1944. Mustang IIIs of No 11 and 13 Groups continued to escort USAAF daylight raids from Britain up to VE-day, and they also covered several of the airborne landings in Europe. Mustang IIIs also served with the Desert Air Force in Italy from the beginning of 1944, replacing Kittyhawks and Hurricanes; their part in breaching the Pescara dam has already been mentioned.

Several Polish squadrons with the RAF flew Mustang IIIs: these were No 306 (Torunski), No 309 (Czerwienski), No 315 (Deblinski) and No 316 (Warszawski) Squadrons. The CO of No 315, Sqn Ldr E. Horbaczewski DFC, Virtuti Militari, Cross of Valour (with three bars) was one of the outstanding Polish fighter pilots and, one day in June 1944, he had led the squadron in a successful attack on German tanks south of Cherbourg. A fellow-pilot was shot down by flak and wounded, and force-landed in a marsh. Horbaczewski, seeing the crashed Mustang, landed successfully at an emergency airstrip being prepared by some Americans nearby, even though it was really too short for a Mustang. He borrowed a jeep from the Americans, drove to the marsh and, wading through water and mud —at times up to his chest—he reached the crashed aircraft and succeeded in extricating the pilot on his own, assisting him back to the jeep. He then got the wounded man to sit on the pilot's seat while he himself sat on the latter's knees and, despite this, took off from the airstrip and flew back safely to England, where the ground crew were astonished to see two men get out of the Mustang's cockpit. Sadly, Horbaczewski was killed in action on 18 August after leading his squadron in an attack on about sixty Focke-Wulf Fw 190s which they

caught taking off from an airfield near Beauvais; he was shot down after himself bringing down three of the Germans, of which sixteen were destroyed altogether. On 9 April 1945 Mustang IIIs of Nos 306 and 309 Squadrons shot down four Messerschmitt Me 262s over Hamburg, these being the Polish fighters' last air victories. And on 25 April Mustangs of Nos 306, 309 and 315 Squadrons formed part of the escort to a force of 255 Lancasters that went to bomb Hitler's mountain retreat at Berchtesgaden; the Mustangs flew a round trip of 1,050 miles in six hours without loss.

Starting with No 19, Mustang IIIs also equipped the following RAF squadrons: Nos 65, 66, 94, 112, 118, 122, 126, 129, 165, 249, 260 and 345, in addition to the Polish units. No 5 Squadron of the South African Air Force also flew Mustang IIIs from September 1944 from bases in Italy.

One of the least-known aspects of the Mustang's service with the RAF was its use by the celebrated No 617 Squadron as a target marker; the CO, Group Captain Leonard Cheshire, had used a Mosquito FB VI on several occasions for this job and it had occurred to him that if a Mosquito was better for marking than a Lancaster, then something even smaller and faster would be better still. He discussed this with his base commander, Air Commodore Sharp, who suggested a P–38 Lightning or a Mustang and then tried to get a Mustang through the Air Ministry. Oddly enough, they were unable to help, and so Sharp decided to fly over to an American base and try to borrow one from the USAAF. He succeeded, and an American pilot flew a Mustang over to Woodhall and explained the cockpit to Cheshire, who had never flown a single-engined fighter or, indeed, any single-engined type since his flying training days back in 1939; moreover, as a bomber pilot, he had not had to do his own navigating for a long time. But there was no time to make a familiarisation flight in the Mustang before No 617 was ordered to attack the Siracourt V–2 rocket site, and it was then found that the smoke markers would not fit the Mustang's underwing racks, so the armourers, working flat out, rigged up a makeshift wire arrangement to hold the markers on.

Cheshire took off half an hour earlier in

A Mustang III of No 260 Sqn with four rocket projectiles under the wings takes off from an Italian airfield (*IWM*)

the Mustang to get the feel of it and embarked on a flight in an unfamiliar aircraft which had to be extremely accurate; his timing over the target had to be within thirty seconds of No 617's Lancasters, and the Mustang cruised about 90mph faster than they did. He had worked out his courses with the help of one of the navigators beforehand, but could not very well work out changes in wind direction as well as map-reading and flying; what is more, he had not tried any practice landings in the Mustang before using it in earnest, in case of an accident, and so had to contend with the added worry of a night landing in an unfamiliar aircraft. But Cheshire soon found the Mustang delightful to fly and within half an hour he had the feel of it. From 7,000ft he dived to 500ft over the concrete slab that protected the underground Siracourt rocket dump and put his smoke bombs within a few feet of the concrete, which was well and truly hit by the Lancasters' 12,000lb 'tallboy' bombs. Cheshire landed the Mustang safely after a magnificent piece of flying, and the mission was a success.

Cheshire flew the Mustang twice more in the same role, on 4 July in a raid on a cave at Creil near Paris that the Germans were using as a store for V–2 rockets and V–1 flying bombs, and the following day to Mimoyecques, site of the huge underground gun barrels trained to fire on London that were Hitler's V–3 secret weapon. Both raids were successful; the entrance to the cave system at Creil was collapsed by the Lancasters' 'tallboys', as were hundreds of yards of the limestone caves themselves, while at Mimoyecques one gun shaft was blocked by a huge piece of concrete, another was collapsed by a near miss and a third was shaken out of plumb.

This was Cheshire's last sortie before being taken off operations with a hundred raids to his credit. His successor as CO of No 617, Wing Commander J. B. Tait DSO, DFC, also used the Mustang for target marking on several occasions. The first time was on a raid to Wizernes where a huge concrete dome 20ft thick on the edge of a chalk quarry protected V–2 rocket stores and launching tunnels leading out of the face of the quarry; this had previously been visited by No 617. On 20 July Tait in the Mustang found broken cloud drifting over the target and thick haze on the ground;

diving through the flak he dropped his smoke markers but, pulling up to 4,000ft, found he could only just see the smoke from there and clearly the bombers, at 18,000ft, would be unable to see it. So Tait did the unprecedented thing of calling up the bombers, instructing them to try and aim at him, and then dived through the bursting flak to circle directly over the great dome at 1,000ft, hoping the glint of his wings would give the bomb aimers a point to aim for. The Mustang shook in the shell blasts and was hit several times, but the bomb aimers still could not see sufficiently so Tait at last pulled out of the flak, luckily unharmed, and the Lancasters brought their 'tallboys' home. They hit this target heavily on a later visit, and when Allied forces captured the launching complex at Wizernes shortly after, they found the 10,000-ton concrete dome knocked off its foundations and long stretches of the launching tunnels and associated galleries caved in.

3 The D-Series Mustang

By mid-1944 the P–51B and P–51C had enjoyed many successes against the Luftwaffe in Europe, and the Merlin-powered Mustang had proved to be superior in speed and manoeuvrability to all German piston-engined fighters above 20,000ft, although Luftwaffe pilots did consider it to be rather vulnerable to cannon fire. Only one shortcoming was causing some concern to the USAAF and likewise the RAF, and that was the lack of rearward vision. The Mustang was not alone in this, however, as several of its contemporaries, notably the Spitfire and the Republic P–47D Thunderbolt, also had this defect and were fitted in their later production forms with 'bubble'-type cockpit canopies. As related earlier, the Mustang's original sideways-hingeing canopy had only limited rear view and the Malcolm bulged canopy, although successfully retrofitted to many P–51Bs, P–51Cs and Mustang IIIs, was really only a stop-gap solution. This rear view problem resulted in a major redesign designated P–51D, in which a large moulded plastic 'bubble'-type sliding canopy was fitted and combined with a cut-down rear fuselage. This canopy was tested on P–51B–1–NA 43–12102, which also had the lowered rear fuselage top line, although the first four production P–51Ds did, in fact, have the old-style canopy. The D-series Mustangs were to be built in larger numbers than any other variant, a total of 6,502 P–51D–NAs being built at Inglewood and 1,454 P–51D–NTs at Dallas. Later production aircraft were fitted with

This P–51B–1–NA 43–12102 was fitted with the P–51D's plastic 'bubble'-type sliding canopy and cut-down rear fuselage to become the prototype P–51D (*RIC*)

a dorsal fin to compensate for the reduction in fuselage side area caused by lowering the top line, and this fin was also retrospectively fitted to many earlier Ds to make them easier to fly on long escort missions. At the same time as the dorsal fin, tail warning radar was also added.

The D had as standard the 1,450hp Packard Merlin V–1650–7 engine fitted to later P–51Bs and P–51Cs, with its higher war emergency rating of 1,695hp at 10,300ft, and the 85 US gal fuselage fuel tank fitted to some P–51Bs and Cs also became standard. Armament was six 0·5in Browning MG 53–2 machine-guns with 270 or 400 rounds per gun, and the last 1,100 P–51D–25–NAs to be built were fitted with twin zero-length launching stubs under the wings for carrying up to ten 5in HVAR rocket projectiles; the initials HVAR stood for High Velocity Aircraft Rocket and six of these rockets and two 500lb or 1,000lb bombs could be carried in the ground attack role. Some P–51Ds in the Pacific area were modified to carry two 500lb depth charges under the wings for anti-submarine patrols in the closing stages of the war. Prior to the 5in HVAR rockets coming into use with the Mustang, some P–51Ds in Europe had been fitted with a cluster of three Bazooka-type rocket-launching tubes under each wing, and often did some ground strafing with rockets or machine-guns when returning from bomber escort flights. P–51D Mustangs of the US 10th Air Force operating in Burma late in 1944 were sometimes fitted with clusters of three rocket-launching tubes and two 1,000lb bombs under the wings for attacking such targets as Japanese water-borne transport in the Myitkina area. Some P–51Ds were also fitted with a 35mm camera gun mounted in the fin to obtain a clearer and wider picture of the target being fired at and the field of fire than was possible with the conventional mounting position; some P–51Ks also had the camera gun mounted in this way. An alternative underwing load sometimes carried by the Mustang was a pair of chemical containers for making a smoke screen.

The first P–51Ds arrived in the United Kingdom in May 1944 and were allotted initially to group and squadron commanders, who needed their improved rear vision the most. As deliveries built up they equipped whole groups and eventually the USAAF equipped all but fifteen of its Fighter Groups with the P–51D, making a total of forty-two Squadrons using this version of the Mustang. All but one of the Eighth Air Force Republic P–47 Thunderbolt groups were eventually re-equipped with the Mustang, which remained a high altitude and escort fighter *par excellence*, although it was used more and more before and after D-Day in the ground attack role shooting up vehicles, trains and dispersed aircraft across France and Germany, often doing ground strafing when returning from bomber escort flights. Mustangs were the only Allied fighters with sufficient range to escort bombers all the way on deep penetration 'shuttle' raids in which landings were made in North Africa or Russia after taking off from United Kingdom or Italian bases. One of the first of these was in May 1944 when P–51s escorted B–17 Fortresses of the US 15th Air Force from Italy on a raid on the Rumanian railway system, going on to land in Russia and being met and escorted into the Soviet Union by Russian fighters; the Russians developed a special long-range version of the Yakovlev Yak–9 known as the Yak–9DD to escort these shuttle raids safely into the Soviet Union. On 21 June 1944 B–17 Fortresses landed at Russian bases after attacking Berlin, being escorted all the way by P–51B Mustangs and met over Poland and escorted into Soviet territory by Yakovlev Yak–9s. Mustangs escorted a number of these shuttle raids, and on one occasion also escorted Lockheed P–38 Lightnings into Russia.

The Mustang's potentialities as a fighter were further enhanced by the new anti-g suits which Eighth Air Force pilots were among the first to wear; these enabled the pilot to 'pull more g' by inflating automatically around his calves, thighs and lower body during tight turns or pull-outs from a dive, preventing the blood from draining away from the head and trunk, and thus delaying the onset of 'black-outs'. But with these suits pilots found they could sometimes take more 'g' than their Mustangs and there were a number of instances after combats when P–51s landed with several degrees more wing dihedral than normal, and a number of popped rivets showing where the wings had bent, and it is a tribute

(*Above*)
Three P–51D Mustangs of the 375th Fighter Sqn,
361st Fighter Group, US 8th Air Force, in
formation with P–51B F2–H in the background
(*USO*)

(*Below*)
Two 1,000lb bombs and six HVAR rocket
projectiles, as seen here on P–51D–5–NA 44–13594,
make up a formidable load for the ground
attack role (*RIC*)

(*Above*)
Some P–51Ds were fitted with a cluster of three Bazooka-type rocket-launching tubes under each wing (*RIC*)

(*Below*)
P–51D G–CY of the 343rd Fighter Sqn, 55th Fighter Group, us 8th Air Force (*via IWM*)

P–51Ds from all four Fighter Groups of the us
15th Air Force: HL–A (rearmost) from the
31st Group, WD–Q 'Queen Marjorie' of the 4th
Fighter Sqn, 52nd Group, '7' of the 100th
Fighter Sqn, and 'OO', the personal aircraft of
Lt Colonel C. H. Beverley, co of the 325th Group
(the 'Checkertail Clan') (*USO*)

to the aircraft's structural design that such
excessive loads did not cause a wing to
come off.

In March 1945 two P–51D Groups, the
15th and the 21st, were sent to Iwo Jima
to escort B–29 Superfortresses on raids
over Japan, and from here they made the
first land-based fighter strikes on Tokyo on
7 April 1945. The Mustang's exceptional
range made it admirably suited to bomber
escort work and fighter sweeps over the
great distances of the Pacific, the P–51D
having an absolute range of no less than
2,080 miles with two 100 us gal drop tanks
giving a total fuel capacity of 489 us gal,
this range representing an endurance of no

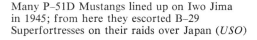

Many P–51D Mustangs lined up on Iwo Jima
in 1945; from here they escorted B–29
Superfortresses on their raids over Japan (*USO*)

less than 8½ hours. Yet it was only in the closing stages of the war that the Mustang was deployed in some numbers to the Pacific theatre where its great range could find the maximum scope, and it is interesting to speculate on the difference it might have made to earlier stages of the Allied campaign in the Pacific had the Allison-engined P–51 or P–51A been put into service in that theatre in 1942 or 1943, even though this might have meant the USAAF taking over some of the RAF Mustang I in order to do so. To take just one example, what a godsend a squadron of P–51s would have been to the defence of Wake Island in that fortnight after Pearl Harbour when a dozen US Marine Corps Grumman F4F–3 Wildcats, eight of their number bombed in the initial Japanese attack, fought heroically to break up Japanese air and sea attacks before the last two were finally destroyed, and the island occupied by the Japs shortly after. Iwo Jima-based P–51Ds were also being used for fighter reconnaissance sorties for the US Navy early in 1945, as well as escorting B–29s to Japan.

Because the USAAF had first priority of P–51D deliveries for the Pacific theatre the RAF received relatively few, a total of 281 being supplied as the Mustang IV, serialled KH641–KH670 and KM493–KM743; a further batch, KM744–KM799, were not delivered. These equipped Nos 19, 64, 65, 112, 118, 122, 213, 249, 303, 442 and 611 Squadrons, most of which had already operated the Mustang III; the Mk IV first entered squadron service in September 1944. No 303 (Kosciuszko's) Squadron was one of

Mustang IV KH774: S–GA of No 112 Sqn, which had flown Curtiss P–40 Kittyhawks with the well-known 'shark's teeth' insignia in the Western Desert and Italy until re-equipping with Mustangs in July 1944; these and subsequent 112 Sqn types up to Hunter jets retained the shark's teeth markings (*IWM*)

(*Right*)
The two-seat trainer version of the P–51D continued to serve after the war, this one being a TF–51D–30–NA with a fixed tailwheel (*RIC*)

the Polish units, and had been one of the top-scoring Polish squadrons in the Battle of Britain. It had started life as the Polish Air Force's 3rd Fighter Squadron at the end of 1919, when it was staffed largely by American volunteers who wanted to repay the debt they owed to the country of Kosciuszko and Pulaski, who had been notable fighters for American independence. The squadron fought against the Bolshevik armies during the war of 1919–20 with Russia and was reformed in Britain in 1940 as No 303, flying Hurricanes initially and later Spitfires. On 16 April 1945 Mustang IVs of No 611 Squadron were the first RAF aircraft to greet aircraft of the Soviet Air Force over Berlin. The Mustang IV remained in RAF service until May 1947, equipping several squadrons in the immediate post-war period. In addition to the Mustang IVs supplied direct from the States, the RAF also took over P–51D–5–NA 44–13332 from the USAAF for evaluation at

50

Boscombe Down, with the British serial TK589; it was later used in the making of an aircraft recognition film. The RAF version of the P–51K–NT was also known as the Mustang IV, in spite of having an Aeroproducts instead of a Hamilton Standard four-blade airscrew and orders for this version were being fulfilled at the end of the war. Serial batches for 593 were allotted, KH671–KH870 and KM100–KM492.

Following the successful in-the-field conversion of P–51B–5–NA 43–6877 to carry General Eisenhower on an inspection flight over the Normandy battlefields shortly after D-Day, a two-seater trainer version of the P–51D was produced, designated TP–51D–NT. This had a second seat, with full dual control, installed behind the normal pilot's seat and in place of the 85 US gal fuel tank, the extra seat being accommodated under the standard 'bubble' cockpit canopy. Unlike almost all other World War II fighters, the Mustang in its two-seater form did not need an extra, stepped cockpit canopy for the second pilot as the existing one was sufficiently large to serve both occupants. To make room for the second pilot, some radio equipment was relocated in the rear fuselage. Altogether ten TP–51D–NT trainer versions were built during the war, serialled 44–84610, 44–84611 and 45–11443 to 45–11450, and they served for a time after the war under the new designation TF–51D–NT; their gross weight was relatively light at 11,300lb. Some more postwar conversions of Ds to TP–51D standard were done by Temco Aircraft Corporation and Cavalier Aircraft. The F–6D–NT was a tactical reconnaissance version, a total of 136 being converted at Dallas from P–51D–NTs to have vertical and oblique camera positions in the rear fuselage. Additional radio was fitted including D/F equipment, and full armament was carried; the gross weight was 11,000lb. After the war the

F–6D was redesignated RF–51D–NT under the new designation system of 11 June 1948, and this version equipped the USAAF National Guard squadrons in the tactical reconnaissance role, supplementing the ANG's F–51D fighter squadrons; under this new designation system the P–51D became the F–51D, and the TRF–51D was a two-seater version of the F–6D. The D was also used as a target tug by the USAAF's 56th Fighter Group during 1947 when it was working up on its new Lockheed P–80A Shooting Star jets, the Mustang towing a 6ft × 30ft target 500ft behind it at 10,000ft for air-to-air firing trials by the P–80As. Figures from this period showed that the 56th did better at air-to-ground firing than air-to-air; in the former category 55 per cent hits were scored out of 11,000 rounds fired, whereas in the air-to-air category only 37 per cent hits out of 45,000 rounds fired were scored by the Group's Shooting Stars.

An F–51D was used after the war as a test bed for the 20in diameter Marquardt 'flying stovepipe' ramjet engine, one of which was fitted at each wing tip; this ramjet was intended for the Martin Gorgon IV air-to-surface winged missile, which was powered by one of these 7ft long engines mounted under its fuselage. At its design speed this Marquardt engine developed the equivalent of 2,500 horsepower, which was sufficient to power a large pilotless aircraft or a small fighter. Ramjets have no moving parts except for a fuel pump and hence cannot be started from rest. At design speeds they have a specific fuel consumption per lb of thrust of perhaps four times that of a non-fan turbojet engine, although much less than a rocket motor; at these speeds the combustion space inside the ramjet is like an inferno in which the heat-release rate exceeds that of any other type of air-breathing engine, and a large thrust is developed for a minimal engine weight. This, and the high fuel consumption at subsonic speeds, limits the ramjet's applications to such fields as missiles and target drones, where the need for very high speeds offsets the disadvantages of high fuel consumption. In the earlier days of ramjets, when the Marquardt 20in engine was flown in the F–51D (it was also flown on an F–82 Twin Mustang), getting the fuel distribution system of these engines right was a major problem, and another big difficulty was the severe vibration that could be excited in flight by the very high power/weight ratios that resulted. Testing in flight by the F–51D and F–82 was especially important because a ramjet could not be tested in a transonic wind tunnel since its exhaust gases would contaminate the air-

KM139 was one of a number of P–51K–NTs being supplied to the RAF as Mustang IVs at the end of the war to supplement the P–51Ds also in service as Mustang IVs (*RIC*)

F–6K–10–NT tactical reconnaissance version 44–12527: QL–L of the 22nd Tactical Reconnaissance Sqn at Speke being prepared for shipment back to the USA at the end of the war, with another F–6K of the same unit behind and P–51Ds of the 343rd Fighter Sqn, 55th Fighter Group and 351st Fighter Sqn, 353rd Fighter Group (*IWM*)

stream. So Roy Marquardt overcame this difficulty in his early days of ramjet design by contracting with a Kaiser Steel company plant to use their blast furnace blower as an air supply, air tapped from the compressor being blown into the mouth of the ramjet at speeds up to 1,000mph.

The next production version of the Mustang to succeed the P–51D immediately was not the P–51H developed from the lightweight XP–51F and XP–51G, but the P–51K–NT. This differed from the D solely in having an Aeroproducts automatic constant-speed four-blade airscrew instead of a Hamilton Standard one, which resulted in a slightly inferior performance to the D's, and in not being fitted with the zero-length rocket-launching stubs under the wings of the last 1,100 P–51D–25–NAs. Altogether 1,337 P–51K–NTs were built at the Dallas plant, and the K version became obsolete in USAAF service fairly soon after the end of the war, the F–51H being preferred to it as post-war first-line equipment for USAAF fighter squadrons. The F–6K–NT, of which 163 were converted at Dallas from P–51Ks, was the tactical reconnaissance version with ports for vertical and oblique cameras in the rear fuselage; this version was otherwise the same as the F–6D–NT, and a few F–6Ks saw brief service in the European theatre of operations, becoming RF–51K–NTs under the new 1948 designation system.

As related in Chapter 5, a small number of P–51Ks, believed to be thirty, were delivered to the Dutch Militaire Luchtvaart (or Military Aviation) after the war to supplement Dutch P–51Ds in service in the East Indies, and for use against the Indonesian nationalist forces. These were the only P–51Ks to be disposed of to a foreign air force after the war, but the Royal Australian Air Force acquired a batch of eighty-four P–51Ks, serialled A68–500 to A68–583, under Lend-Lease from the States at the end of the war to supplement 214 similarly acquired P–51Ds; these were to fill the gap until Australian production of the Mustang by Commonwealth Aircraft Corporation Pty Ltd could get into its stride. Mustang production at the Dallas plant ceased after VJ Day with the last P–51K to come off the line, but production continued at Inglewood until November 1945 when the last of 15,586 Mustangs to be built, a P–51H, was completed; contracts for a further 5,973 Mustangs were cancelled after VJ Day. The P–82 Twin Mustang succeeded the P–51H on the Inglewood production lines and it was able to use a good many of the existing Mustang jigs and tooling. By VJ Day the USAAF had 5,500 Mustangs in service and the RAF and other Commonwealth air forces had another 1,300 in use.

4 Lightweight and other Versions

The designation P–51E was not used, and after the P–51D design effort now concentrated on lightening the Mustang for, although not as massive and heavy a fighter as the Republic P–47 Thunderbolt which, in its final production P–47N form weighed 21,200lb loaded, the P–51D's maximum loaded weight of 11,600lb with drop tanks was still about a ton heavier than the Spitfire IX's. Three lightweight versions of the P–51D were produced experimentally, the XP–51F, XP–51G and XP–51J, culminating in the production of P–51H which was, in fact, the last version of the Mustang to be built. The XP–51F was extensively redesigned through simplifying the structure to a combination of optimum British and American strength requirements, using some new materials such as plastics for such parts as access doors, and deleting some equipment. A new low-drag laminar flow wing was designed for the XP–51F, and smaller wheels and tyres were fitted with new disc brakes; these resulted in the slight forward

The prototype XP–51F, one of three lightweight versions of the Mustang. This view shows how the smaller wheels and tyres have eliminated the slight forward sweep at the inner wing leading edges of all previous Mustangs. The XP–51F had a very smooth finish achieved by a special glazed putty covering (*RIC*)

sweep at the inner wing leading edges that had been characteristic of all previous Mustangs being dispensed with, while the undercarriage itself was simplified and lightened. To reduce drag the bubble cockpit canopy was made longer, while a new pilot's seat of thick armour plate, with a rubber back-rest and a metal bucket for the parachute, was fitted; the cockpit layout was simplified. The same 1,450hp Packard Merlin V–1650–7 engine as the P–51D's was fitted, being carried on lightened engine mountings, and the cowling was redesigned. The ventral radiator fairing was modified, with the oil cooler replaced by a heat exchanger, and the fuel system was redesigned around two 105 us gal wing tanks. The P–51D's four-blade prop was replaced by a three-blade Aeroproducts Unimatic hydraulic constant speed airscrew with wide chord hollow steel blades to save more weight.

The whole hydraulic system was reworked and simplified, armament was reduced from six to four 0·5in Browning MG 53–2 machine-guns and the dorsal fin was removed. All these changes combined to reduce the gross weight by about 1 ton to 9,060lb, and the empty weight to 5,635lb from the P–51D's 7,125lb. A very smooth finish was achieved by a special glazed

One of the three XP–51Fs built was supplied to the RAF for evaluation with the serial FR409, and finished in standard day fighter camouflage (*IWM*)

putty covering developed at North American, and this made the XP–51F the fastest Mustang to date, with a maximum speed of 466mph at 29,000ft. Three of this version were built, serialled 43–43332, 43–43333 and 43–43334, and one of these was supplied to the RAF for evaluation, being taken on charge in June 1944 with the serial FR409. Rather surprisingly, it was finished in standard day fighter camouflage, thereby losing something in top speed, and the lightweight F version would have been known as the Mustang V had it been ordered for the RAF.

The second lightweight version was the XP–51G, very similar to the XP–51F but powered by a 1,500hp (maximum take-off) Rolls-Royce RM14SM Merlin 145 driving

The XP–51G was very similar to the XP–51F but powered by a British-built Rolls-Royce RM14SM Merlin 145 driving a five-blade Rotol airscrew (*RIC*)

a five-blade Rotol airscrew; this version of the Merlin fitted was a British-built engine as Packard did not then manufacture it, but were due to start making the RM14SM series of Merlins when these had gone into production in the UK. The gross weight was only 8,879lb, almost as light as the first production P–51, and the maximum speed was 472mph at 20,750ft. Two XP–51Gs were built, 43–43335 and 43–43336, and one of these became FR410 for evaluation by the RAF. The third lightweight, the XP–51J, was the first Mustang since the P–51A to have an Allison V–1710 engine; its powerplant was the 1,500hp (maximum take-off) V–1710–119 which increased the length by some 8in to 32ft 11in. It was otherwise similar to the XP–51F, but the carburettor

The lightweight XP–51G was the only Mustang to have a five-blade airscrew (*RIC*)

The third lightweight version, the XP–51J, had an Allison V–1710–119 engine, being the first Allison-engined Mustang since the P–51A and A–36A, and was the fastest of the three lightweights (*RIC*)

air intake was removed from underneath the cowling to be incorporated in the ventral radiator scoop, thus giving a very clean cowling shape. The gross weight was down to 9,141lb and the airscrew was a three-blade Aeroproducts one similar to the XP–51F's. The XP–51J was very fast, reaching a maximum speed of 491mph at 27,400ft with water injection, and its service ceiling was 43,700ft, this later supercharged version of the Allison engine having the high-altitude performance that the earlier V–1710s fitted to the P–51, P–51A and Mustang I had lacked. Two XP–51Js were built, serialled 44–76027 and 44–76028.

From the XP–51F was evolved the production lightweight version of the Mustang, the P–51H–NA, which appeared near the end of 1944. This had a 1,380hp (maximum take-off) Packard Merlin V–1650–9 which gave a maximum of 2,220hp at 10,200ft with water injection under its war emergency rating. The P–51H featured a taller fin and rudder with dorsal extension to improve directional stability and the aircraft's steadiness as a gun platform, although the first twenty-four P–51Hs to be built had the standard P–51D vertical tail surfaces without the dorsal fin. The fuselage was slightly longer, giving an overall length of 33ft 4in, and the bubble cockpit canopy was shorter than the XP–51F's. The same shallower carburettor air intake as the XP–51F's was featured, as well as the modified engine cowling, and a four-blade Aeroproducts automatic constant-speed airscrew was fitted. The two 105 us gal wing tanks of the

XP–51F were supplemented by a 50 us gal fuselage fuel tank, to give a fuel capacity of 260gal. Armament was four or six 0·5in Browning MG 53–2 machine-guns, and up to ten 5in rocket projectiles could be carried under the wings on twin zero-length launching stubs, as well as the same bombs or drop tanks as on the P–51D. The H's maximum overload weight, at 10,500lb, was about half a ton less than the P–51D's, and its maximum speed of 487mph at 25,000ft made it the fastest production version of the Mustang. This was exactly 100mph faster at an altitude 10,000ft higher than the initial production P–51 of 1941—a graphic illustration of just what development potential the Merlin engine combined with some structural redesign and lightening had made possible; certainly few, if any, other World War II fighters achieved the performance increase of the Mustang between its first and last production versions.

Altogether 2,000 P–51Hs were ordered but only 555 were built, the remaining 1,445 being cancelled after VJ Day. One of these, serialled KN987, was supplied to the RAF for evaluation. The H was too late to take part in fighter operations over Europe but it did equip a number of fighter groups in the

The P–51H was the production lightweight version of the Mustang, and had a taller fin and rudder to improve its steadiness as a gun platform, although the first twenty-four P–51Hs to be built originally had standard P–51D vertical tail surfaces. The H was the fastest production version of the Mustang; the second of 555 built is seen here (*RIC*)

Pacific in the closing months of the war, and was first-line equipment in both USAAF and National Guard squadrons in the early post-war years. Had the war continued into 1946–7, two more versions of the Mustang were scheduled to go into production, the P–51L–NA and the P–51M–NT. The former was the same as the P–51H, but powered by a 1,500hp (maximum take-off) Packard Merlin V–1650–11 engine and with an over-all length of 33ft 4in. 1,700 P–51Ls were ordered but cancelled after VJ Day, and none of this version were built. The P–51M, to have been built at the Dallas plant and of which 1,628 were cancelled after VJ Day, differed from the P–51H only in having a 1,400hp (maximum take-off) Packard Merlin V–1650–9A engine and a gross weight of 11,000lb. One P–51M–1–NT, serialled 45–11743, was completed before the axe fell on production plans for this version.

Australian production

The Royal Australian Air Force had already used Mustang IIIs and IVs along-side the RAF in Italy since November 1944, No 3 Squadron replacing its Kittyhawks with Mustangs of both these marks on the 17th of that month, and flying them from their base at Fano on the coast on sorties across the Adriatic in support of the parti-sans in Yugoslavia, often carrying two

P–51Hs were first-line equipment in both USAF and National Guard squadrons in the early post-war years (*RIC*)

500lb bombs. These aircraft had RAF serials, but the type's major usefulness to the RAAF was intended to be in the Pacific theatre, where its exceptional range could be used to best advantage. To this end a licence to build the P–51D in Australia was acquired by Commonwealth Aircraft Corporation Pty Ltd – CAC, which had earlier built under licence from North American 755 examples of a developed general-purpose version of the NA–16–1 advanced trainer known as the Wirraway, the first of which had been delivered to the RAAF in July 1939. Tooling up for the Mustang at CAC's Fisher-man's Bend plant near Melbourne began in February 1945 and imported parts for 100 were provided by North American, of which 80 were assembled into complete aircraft and the remaining 20 sets of components were used to set up the production line.

The first Australian-manufactured P–51D, known as the CA–17 Mustang 20, flew on 29 April 1945, but Commonwealth-built aircraft were just too late to partici-pate in the war against Japan. Originally 250 were to have been built by CAC, but only 200 were finally completed. The first 80, with RAAF serials A68–1 to A68–80, were Mustang 20s powered by a 1,520hp Packard Merlin V–1650–3 engine, and they were followed by a second batch of 120, designated CA–18 by Commonwealth, of which 170 had originally been ordered. Of these, the first 40 were Mustang 21s serialled A68–81 to A68–120, with 1,450hp Packard Merlin V–1650–7 (Merlin 68) engines. The first 14 of these, A68–81 to A68–94, were

fitted with an F.24 oblique-facing camera in the fuselage and redesignated Mustang 22s; a second batch of 14 Mk 22s, A68–187 to A68–200, brought production to an end, following a batch of 66 Mustang 23s (A68–121 to A68–186) which differed from the earlier marks in having British-built Merlin 66 or 70 engines. Contracts for a further 250 Mustangs designated CA–21 by Commonwealth were cancelled after the war. The RAAF also acquired a total of 298 Mustangs from the USA under Lend-Lease, a batch of 84 P–51Ks, serialled A68–500 to A68–583, and A68–600 to A68–813, which were P–51Ds. One other Mustang was also acquired as a pattern aircraft for the Australian production line and given the serial A68–1001.

Some of the P–51Ds that were used by No 77 Squadron in Korea were afterwards disposed of to the Republic of Korea Air Force when No 77 re-equipped with Gloster Meteor F.8s in 1951. The Mustang's first duty with the post-war RAAF was serving with the British Commonwealth Occupation Force in Japan and No 81 Wing, consisting of Nos 76, 77 and 82 Squadrons, then based at Labuan, British North Borneo, and in the process of re-equipping with Mustangs, was chosen for this task. The Wing left Labuan for its main base at Iwakuni in Japan in February and March 1946, spending an initial period at Bofu until the airfield at Iwakuni had been made usable. From here patrols were flown over different areas

P–51D Mustangs were built under licence in Australia by Commonwealth Aircraft Corp at Fishermen's Bend, near Melbourne, where 200 were produced. Most had Packard Merlins but these two, A68–182 and A68–181, were part of a batch of 66 Mustang 23s with British-built Merlin 66 or 70 engines (*IWM*)

of Japan on surveillance duties, and in 1949 Nos 76 and 82 Squadrons were withdrawn. As related in Chapter 5, No 77 stayed on and saw plenty of action in Korea in the ground strafing and escort roles, its Mustangs being replaced by Meteors in May 1951.

The Mustang's other main task in RAAF service was equipping the Citizen Air Force, equivalent to Britain's RAF Volunteer Reserve, which it was announced in 1948 was to be reformed in the capital cities of each state. Five fighter squadrons were accordingly formed, each of which had a few Wirraway trainers as well as Mustangs, and they were: No 21 (City of Melbourne), based at Laverton Victoria, No 22 (City of Sydney) based at Richmond, New South Wales, No 23 (City of Brisbane), based at Archerfield, Queensland, No 24 (City of Adelaide), based at Parafield, South Australia, and No 25 (City of Perth), based at Pearce, Western Australia. Mustangs equipped these squadrons until the late 1950s when they were replaced by Meteor F.8s in Nos 22 and 23 Squadrons and by de Havilland Vampires in Nos 21 and 25; No 24 Squadron retained its Mustangs until June 1960 when the five Citizen Air Force squadrons changed over to a non-flying role, being affiliated to one of the permanent RAAF squadrons and training with it. Mustangs and Vampire trainers also equipped No 2 Operational Training Unit at Williamstown, Victoria.

Several Mustangs later came on to the Australian civil register and by 1962 seven were current: Mk 21 VH–AUB (ex–A68–107), owned by A. J. R. Oates of Bathurst, New South Wales; Mk 20 VH–BOY (ex–A68–39) and Mk 22 VH–BOZ (ex–A68–199), owned by the Illawarra Flying School (Air Training Pty Ltd) of Bankstown, near Sydney; Mk 21 VH–BOW (ex–A68–107), owned by Fawcett Aviation; Mk 22 VH–FCB (ex–A68–192), owned by F. C. Braund of Tamworth, New South Wales; Mk 21 VH–UWB (ex–A68–113), owned by J. W. Brookes of the Civil Flying School Ltd, Moorabbin Airport, Victoria; and Mk 21 VH–WAS (ex–A68–118), owned by Wilmore Aviation Services Pty Ltd of Sydney.

Another Australian Mustang 20, VH–BVM (ex–A68–5), registered in 1955, had been acquired by the British racing driver Ron Flockhart in 1961 and registered G–ARKD for an attempt on the Sydney–London record set up in March 1938 by Flying Officer (later Group Captain) A. E. Clouston and Victor Ricketts in the de Havilland DH 88 Comet G–ACSS, one of eleven records broken in ten days in their flight from Gravesend to Blenheim in New Zealand and back to Croydon. Ron Flockhart left Sydney in Mustang G–ARKD on his attempt on 28 February 1961 but mechanical trouble forced him to land at Athens where the attempt was called off on 4 March. This was all the more disappointing as the aircraft had only done 100 hours flying over a six-year period as VH–BVM before Flockhart bought it; it was later cancelled from the register after being damaged beyond repair following a fire in its cockpit during overhaul work at Athens on 7 September that year. In its place a second Mustang, VH–UWB (ex–A68–113) was acquired for another attempt on the record, and was registered G–ARUK. The departure from Sydney was scheduled for 16 April 1962 but, tragically, Ron Flockhart was killed in this Mustang on the 12th when he crashed into high ground near Kallista, in the Dandenong Ranges, in Victoria when flying from Melbourne to Sydney.

Another Australian Mustang lost in an accident was VH–IVI, which carried the legend 'Sydney & Suburban Car Rentals' under the cockpit; this dived vertically into the ground at Windsor, New South Wales, on 11 June 1973 killing the pilot. Two RAAF Mustangs that were never converted to civil use had been acquired by Adastra Airways in the early 1960s, apparently as a source of spares by the owner of VH–FCB, who worked for this small airline; they were Mk 21 A68–104 and Mk 22 A68–187. During 1971–2 work started on modifying the latter to take a Rolls-Royce Dart turboprop from an Ansett–ANA or a Trans-Australia Airlines Vickers Viscount; both airlines had by then retired their fleets of Viscounts, and a number of them had been broken up. This Dart installation would have been similar to the one developed by Cavalier Aircraft for the Turbo Mustang 3, as related in Chapter 5, but problems arose with it, and the Mustang was later taken to Canberra, where it was intended to fit another Dart taken from a Fokker F.27 Friendship airliner. But in the end this project did not come to fruition and the proposed Dart-engined Mustang never received Australian Department of Civil Aviation approval.

Deck landing trials

Another little-known aspect of the Mustang's career is its completion of successful deck landing trials on board the US Navy carrier *Shangri La*. Preliminary tests of the P–51D as a shipborne aircraft had started in early or mid-1944, initial flight tests being begun at the Inglewood plant by North American's engineering test pilot R. C. 'Bob' Chilton, and the aircraft used was P–51D–25–NA 44–94900, which featured strengthened inboard wing panels and a taller fin and rudder similar to that of the P–51H but of slightly broader chord; strengthening in the form of extra plates was added to the wing upper surfaces over the ammunition boxes. The results of these tests making simulated deck landings were successful, and an arrester hook was not fitted. This Mustang was later redesignated an ETF–51D–25–NA and used for high speed research, and later still it came on to the strength of the 148th Fighter Inter-

Flown by Lt R. M. Elder USN, P–51D–5–NA
Mustang 44–14017 is seen here about to take off
from the US carrier *Shangri La* in the course of
deck landing trials (*NLA*)

ception Squadron of the Pennsylvania National Guard who used it in the normal fighter role with the serial 0–484900; it retained its non-standard vertical tail surfaces and inner wing structure, and was now designated a TF–51D–25–NA.

The favourable results of simulated deck landing tests were followed up on the carrier *Shangri La* using P–51D–5–NA 44–14017 which was fitted with an arrestor hook under the extreme rear fuselage aft of the tailwheel bay and a few associated structural modifications were made at North American's Dallas plant. When this work was completed and tested the P–51D was flown to the Norfolk Navy Yard in Virginia and the Philadelphia Navy Yard, Pennsylvania, for ground catapult tests. These proved to be so successful that plans for further catapult tests at sea were abandoned as unnecessary. The 27,100 ton carrier *Shangri La*, which had an overall length of 855ft 10in, left the Norfolk Navy Yard on the evening of 13 November 1944 and proceeded to a point about 85 miles east of Chesapeake Bay. Piloted by Lt R. M. Elder, US Navy, the Mustang arrived on schedule at 11.30 the following morning and, after the carrier had headed into wind, Lt Elder made a 90mph approach and executed an excellent landing, being cheered by hundreds of the ship's personnel, all of whom had been allowed to witness these tests by the *Shangri La*'s captain to mark this special occasion; the ship had been commissioned only two months previously. Lt Elder made four more landings and take-offs, all completely successful; the first take-off was from the 700ft line, and although in the excitement of the moment the pilot failed to trim the aircraft properly, the Mustang took off promptly. The second take-off began at the 600ft line and after a run of only 250ft the Mustang was airborne; this bore out the claims of North American's engineering representatives on board that if the carrier's speed provided a 35 knot headwind over the deck then the take-off run would not exceed 600ft. On landing, with the aircraft at a gross weight of 9,600lb, the maximum runout of the deck arrestor cable was 82ft. Lt Elder flew the Mustang back to the Norfolk Navy Yard after completion of these highly successful initial trials, and it was then scheduled to perform a series of severe off-centre landings at the Philadelphia Navy Yard.

The Mustang's wide-track undercarriage, good handling qualities and exceptional range would have made it an excellent carrier-based fighter, and North American in fact did design studies of carrier-based versions of other P–51 variants, including the P–51H, with an arrestor hook and wing-folding mechanism for the folding wing-tips. By contrast, the Chance Vought Corsair, although designed as a carrier-based fighter, was considered unsuitable by the US Navy for shipborne operations for a long time. The first carrier-based squadron, VMF–124, did not begin operations from the USS *Essex* until 28 December 1944, although Corsairs had been very successful as land-based fighters in the Pacific island campaigns since April 1943. Early in 1944 comparative trials had been flown between the Corsair in F4U–1 and F4U–1A versions and a P–51B Mustang to determine the latter's suitability for naval use; the P–51B was flown at a weight of 9,423lb compared with the 12,162lb of the two Corsairs. The latter had an equal range to the Mustang but nearly twice the firepower, and the F4U–1 proved to be faster than the P–51B at most altitudes up to 24,200ft, above which height the P–51B had the edge, achieving a true air speed of 450mph at 30,000ft. The Corsairs had a better climb rate to 20,000ft, above which the P–51B was superior, and were much better than the Mustang in level flight acceleration, manoeuvrability and response, with a better take-off performance and lower stalling speed, although the Mustang had a better dive acceleration. But the Mustang's lateral control at low speeds was felt to be inade-quate for carrier-based operations, and forward visibility over the nose in the three-point landing attitude was very poor —although the latter criticism was one that could be levelled at almost any naval fighter with a liquid-cooled, in-line engine; this had also been a serious fault of the F4U–1 Corsair, and to cure it the cabin had been raised 7in on later production F4U–1s, which also had a new clear-view cockpit canopy. For these reasons the Mustang was not ordered by the US Navy, in spite of its successful carrier trials.

Another Mustang briefly associated with the US Navy for a time was the P–51H–5–NA 44–64192 used on bailment contract to the Navy with the serial BuAer 09054 for use by Grumman. It was employed by them to flight-test certain aerodynamic features of the XF10F–1 jet fighter, an experimental design which did pass prototype stage.

5 The Post-War Story

Mustang production at the Dallas plant had ceased after VJ Day, but it continued a little while longer at Inglewood until November 1945 when the last of 15,586 to be built, a P–51H, was completed. The P–82 Twin Mustang followed on the Inglewood production lines, and when the 'F' prefix for fighters superseded the old 'P' (for Pursuit) in USAAF designations on 11 June 1948 the two types became respectively the F–51 and F–82. Both the F–51D–NA and F–51H–NA were first-line equipment in the US Air Force on 1 January 1949 while a few ZF–51B–NAs (ex–P–51Bs) and ZF–51K–NTs (ex–P–51Ks) were still in service; the 'Z' prefix denoted obsolete status and 'a few' in this context meant that three or more examples of these versions were still on the USAF List. The RF–51D–NT (formerly F–6D–NT) was still second-line equipment, as was the TF–51D–NT trainer, and a few RF–51K–NTs (formerly F–6K–NTs) were still in use; under the new designation system of 11 June 1948 the photo reconnaissance F–6D and F–6K were redesignated, along with versions of a number of other types, to eliminate multiple designations for one basic aeroplane used in a variety of roles.

F–51Ds and F–51Hs, as well as Republic F–47 Thunderbolts, formed the initial first-line equipment of the USAF National Guard fighter squadrons, which usually had twenty-five aircraft each, while the Guard's photo recce squadrons used the RF–51D–NT. The Air National Guard is a part-time volunteer reserve very similar in basic concept to the British RAFVR, organised on a territorial basis (in this case by states) and in which personnel had to put in certain compulsory minimum periods of drill or flying hours per month. By 1963 the National Guard was contributing over sixty units of various types to the main USAF operation Commands. The Korean War saw Mustangs used not only by the USAF but by the South African Air Force and the Royal Australian Air Force, and F–82 Twin Mustang night fighters also served in Korea, the USAF's last remaining F–51s being withdrawn from service in that country in February 1953, five months before the armistice was signed

bringing an end to that conflict. When the Korean War had broken out in June 1950 many USAF Air Defence Command aircraft and squadrons were sent to the Far East, and the National Guard units, which had been in the process of re-equipping with F–86 Sabre jets, had many of their more modern aircraft, particularly Sabres, taken away to reinforce other USAF units, and had to make do for a time with older types such as F–51 Mustangs, Lockheed F–80 Shooting Stars and Republic F–84 Thunderjets. Mustang IVs had remained in service with RAF Fighter Command until May 1947, but several Commonwealth countries which had used the Mustang in the closing stages of the war, in particular Australia, Canada and South Africa, operated it for several years after hostilities ceased.

Mustangs with foreign air forces

The war had not yet ended before surplus USAAF Mustangs began to be supplied to foreign air forces, both of America's allies like Nationalist China and France, and of neutral Sweden, the first of a number of countries to choose the type to re-equip their air forces with something more modern. Fifty P–51Ds were supplied to the Chinese Nationalist Air Force before VJ Day and by March 1948, under the US Aid Programme to China, 936 aircraft of different types had been delivered with the aim of establishing eight Groups and one-third of a ninth in the Chinese Air Force, and 135 more were still to come, these including B–24 Liberators, P–47 Thunderbolts, C–46 Commando transports and another batch of 53 P–51D Mustangs. On the cessation of hostilities in the Far East in 1945 General Chiang Kai-shek's government had bought the entire surplus stock of about 1,000 USAAF aircraft in that theatre, and these doubtless included a number of P–51Bs that had served with the US 14th Air Force in China, as well as some P–51Ds. It is not known how many of these were made serviceable and put back into operations against the advancing Communist forces; the Chinese Air Force was reorganised after the war and suffered from a shortage of trained maintenance

One of fifty P–51D Mustangs supplied to the Chinese Nationalist Air Force before VJ Day on test before delivery (*USO*)

personnel. And as the civil war situation deteriorated and the Nationalists were seen to be losing their hold on the Chinese mainland, it was not surprising if officers and other ranks changed their loyalties to the winning Communist side. At least one P–51D—and possibly enough for a squadron or two—captured from the Nationalists was flown later in the markings of the Peoples' Republic of China Air Force.

France also acquired a number of P–51Ds for l'Armée de l'Air's reconnaissance wing, the 33ème Escadre de Reconnaissance. The 2/33 Savoie escadron (squadron) was, in February 1945, the first unit of the wing to re-equip with the P–51D for tactical reconnaissance and it joined the 1/33 Belfort escadron, the wing's other squadron, at Colmar; on 5 May that year the 33ème Escadre moved to Freiburg-im-Breisgau in southern Germany where it stayed until May 1950 when it changed its base to

Cognac. The first Republic F–84G Thunderjets arrived to replace the Mustangs in August 1952.

The Royal Swedish Air Force (or Flygvapnet, as it was known) had started to take an interest in the Mustang as the result of two P–51B–5–NAs force-landing in that country and being interned. They were taken over by Flygvapnet under the designation J 26 and flown by the Swedes for evaluation; they were given the Swedish serials 26001 (ex 43–6365 'Z Hub') and 26002 (ex 43–6461 'Hot Pants'). Two more interned P–51D–5–NTs were similarly taken over by Flygvapnet and test flown with the serials 26003 (ex 44–13345) and 26004 (ex 44–13917). These had belonged to the 357th and 339th Fighter Groups respectively. As a result of flying the interned examples, the Swedes liked the Mustang sufficiently to place an initial order with the US Government in April 1945 for 50 surplus P–51Ds, and they eventually acquired a total of 157 P–51Ds in all, which had the Swedish serials 26005–26161; these were designated J 26

In the static display at the Swedish Air Force museum at F 3 wing's base at Malmen is 26020, one of the 157 P–51D Mustangs acquired by Sweden during 1945–8. This one, formerly P–51D–20–NA 44–63992, was sold to the Israeli Air Force in 1952 and was later returned by the Israelis for restoration as a museum piece at the beginning of 1966 (*Aviation Photo News via AP*)

under the Flygvapnet designation system and the first 28 had already been delivered by 13 April 1945, being flown from Germany by US pilots. The J 26s equipped F 16 'Upplands' wing (or Flygflottilj) at Uppsala and the F 4 'Jämtlands' wing at Frösön, and later at Östersund. The last P–51Ds were not delivered until March 1948 and in 1951 12 of the J 26s were fitted with a camera for photo reconnaissance and redesignated S 26 in their new role; they served with F 21 wing at Luleå.

In 1952 the Swedes sold 42 of their J 26 Mustangs to the Dominican Air Force and in September that year signed a contract for the sale of 25 more to the Israeli Defence Force/Air Force. In November 1954 26 more J 26s were sold to Nicaragua for that country's air force. Exactly ten years later the Swedish Aviation Historical Society approached the Israeli Air Force with a view to obtaining one of its now-surplus P–51Ds for exhibition at the Swedish Air Force museum. The Israelis were willing to spare one and this was dismantled, crated and transported to Haifa, arriving at the port of Gothenburg on 7 January 1966. It was then taken to F 9 wing, near Gothenburg, for restoration and it finally appeared in its original Flygvapnet markings and serial 26020 (ex P–51D–20–NA 44–63992).

It now bears F 16 wing insignia and a special squadron badge, and is displayed at the Swedish Air Force museum at F 3 wing's base at Malmen.

The Israeli Air Force's twenty-five Mustangs were delivered from Sweden from November 1952 to June 1953 and were employed both as fighters and as ground attack aircraft, playing a successful part in the 1956 Sinai campaign against Egypt, in the ground attack role. As a result of this campaign it was decided by the Israeli Air Force to phase out all piston-engined aircraft from first-line or second-line service, but it was not until 1960 that the Mustangs were finally retired. The sale of Mustangs to Israel by Sweden was a rare exception to the latter's traditionally neutralist policy of not engaging in arms deals with countries in politically sensitive areas like the Middle East liable to erupt into conflict.

The unit of forty-two former Swedish J 26s supplied to the Dominican Air Force (El Cuerpo de Aviacion Militar Dominicana)

Coded '11', this is one of the twenty-five Swedish Air Force P–51Ds acquired by the Israeli Defence Force/Air Force; note zero-length rocket-launching stubs outside underwing 'stores' pylon (*CWC*)

One of twenty-six ex-Swedish Air Force P–51Ds sold to the Fuerza Aerea Nicaraguense (Nicaraguan Army Air Force). This one does not have the standard Nicaraguan roundels but does feature that country's blue and white rudder stripes; note fabric missing from bottom of rudder (*HH*)

equipped its one fighter-bomber squadron, the Escuadron de Caza. About thirty of the ones still in service were overhauled and updated by Trans-Florida Aviation Inc in 1965, but by 1978 the number surviving had dwindled to just over a dozen, and budget restrictions on the Fuerza Aérea Dominicana (as this air arm was now named) did not provide for their replacement or further modernisation. The twenty-six ex-Swedish Mustangs sold to the Nicaraguan Army Air

Force (Fuerza Aérea Nicaraguense) in November 1954 served until 1965, when a number of them were sold to the Maco Sales Financial Corporation in the USA, and some of these later acquired US civil registrations.

Several of the other Caribbean countries had acquired surplus P–51D Mustangs as a result of military aid or treaty agreements with the USA. Cuba's air force was known under President Batista's regime as the Cuban Aviation Corps, or Cuerpo de Aviacion, and it received a few P–51Ds under the Rio Pact of September 1947; known in full as the Inter-American Treaty of Reciprocal Assistance, and signed by all the Latin American countries and the USA, this provided for collective self-defence should any of the member states be attacked by an external power, and also for the peaceful settlement of disputes between themselves. Cuba withdrew from this treaty in March 1960 and the Cuban Mustangs, which had remained in service until well into the 1950s, were, with other types, replaced when the air force was completely re-equipped from 1960 with Russian types. A few F–51Ds were acquired by the Corps d'Aviation d'Haiti in the 1950s and six of them now equip this air arm's sole fighter-bomber unit; these were previously part of a composite squadron with various training types such as the North American T–6 Texan. The Guatemalan Air Force (Fuerza Aerea de Guatemala) operated one squadron of eleven F–51D fighter-bombers supplied by the USA in 1955 under the Military Assistance Programme, but the last six of these were returned to the USA late in 1972 after the squadron re-equipped with Cessna A–37B jets for COIN (counter-insurgency) duties. These six had originally served with the 109th Fighter Squadron of the Minnesota Air National Guard before going to Guatemala, and were acquired in 1972 by Colonel Don Hull of the Confederate Air Force for restoration.

The Football War
In 1969 Mustangs were involved in the short-lived and little known conflict between Honduras and El Salvador that must surely rank as the first ever Football War (but will it be the last?), so called because the incident that started the flare-up between the two countries occurred in May 1969

during World Cup elimination matches between Honduras and Salvador. During the first two matches in a three-game series to determine which country should go forward in the World Cup series, citizens of both countries fought both on and off the field, and after the second match Honduras broke off diplomatic relations with El Salvador. World Cup officials ordered that the deciding game be played in neutral Mexico City and El Salvador won this on 27 June. Relations between the two countries continued to simmer and the Hondurans claimed that El Salvadorean troops invaded their territory on 14 July and that her Mustangs had swept in on what was described as a 'Pearl Harbour-type' attack on seven Honduran towns. The Fuerza Aerea Salvadoreña had recently acquired six refurbished F–51D Mustangs to supplement its only combat unit, a flight of F4U–4 Corsair fighter-bombers. Reports spoke of heavy civilian casualties in two of the Honduran towns bombed, Santa de Coman and Ocotepeque, and four Salvadorean aircraft were said to have been shot down. The Honduran Air Force (Fuerza Aérea Hondureña) also operated Corsairs of the F4U–4, F4U–5 and F4U–5N versions, and these were used in a reprisal bombing raid over El Salvador that put San Salvador's Ilopanga Airport temporarily out of action and destroyed the Acajutla oil refinery on the country's Pacific coast; the Corsairs were met by heavy anti-aircraft fire. El Salvador's National Assembly declared a state of siege, suspended all school classes and threatened to bomb Tegucigalpa, the Honduran capital, if Honduras bombed civilians. The Government in a broadcast to the people claimed that El Salvador had 118 planes ready for combat—a total far in excess of their diminutive air force, and which presumably included every single light aircraft and airliner registered in the country that could have been used under military command. It went on to say: 'For each bomb the Honduran Air Force discharges on San Salvador or on any other city against civilians, El Salvador will drop 10 bombs on Tegucigalpa'. Brave words but—luckily for the civilians—neither country was equipped with light bombers such as Douglas B–26 Invaders or North American B–25 Mitchells like some Central American republics.

This led to the Salvadorean Air Force using Douglas DC–3s, of which it had two or three, as makeshift bombers on at least one raid over Tegucigalpa; an eye-witness related how the Salvadorean planes circled low over their target and crew members could be seen opening the cargo doors and manually pushing the bombs out; there was no attempt at sighting the bombs and little attempt to hit specific targets. (The year before, the Nigerian Air Force had also used DC–3s as makeshift bombers in a similar way over the Uli airstrip in an attempt to stop the Super Constellations flying supplies into Biafra.) Fierce fighting was also taking place along the border between Honduras and El Salvador, with incursions by both countries into the other's territory and casualties on both sides. Relations between the two countries had been tense for several years before this conflict erupted, the root cause of antagonism being El Salvador's need for *lebensraum*; with an area of 8,260 square miles (about the same as Israel) and a population of 3,100,000, Salvador was only one-fifth the size of neighbouring Honduras with its

2,500,000 people. It was, in fact, the smallest and most densely populated country in Central America, and in recent years thousands of Salvadoreans had crossed the border into Honduras in search of farming land; their presence there had led to some ill-feeling between the two countries. In 1975 the six F–51D Mustangs remaining in the Fuerza Aerea Salvadoreña were replaced by Israeli-built CM.170 Magister strike/trainers; ironically enough both countries have re-equipped their small air forces significantly, in the light of the recurring clashes between them, in the last few years with Israel's help, which has taken the form of Arava light transports and ex-Israeli Air Force jet fighters.

The Uruguayan Air Force (Fuerza Aérea Uruguaya) acquired twenty-five ex-USAF P–51Ds in 1950 and these equipped its one fighter squadron, the Grupo 2-Caza, until replaced by Lockheed F–80C Shooting Stars from 1958. Six F–51Ds were sold to the Fuerza Aérea Boliviano (Bolivian Air Force) in 1960 and, together with four others acquired elsewhere, formed the sole Bolivian fighter-bomber squadron; a second strike/attack squadron has recently been formed with armed AT–6D and T–28A/D trainers, and Brazilian-built versions of the Aermacchi MB.326 strike trainer are also in service. The Mustangs were used until 1977 for COIN duties and have been overhauled and updated by Cavalier Aircraft Corpora-

One of twenty-five P–51D Mustangs acquired by the Uruguayan Air Force (Fuerza Aerea Uruguaya) in 1950, these equipping its one fighter squadron, the Grupo 2–Caza, which began to re-equip with F–80C Shooting Star jets in 1958. The Mustangs were finally withdrawn in 1960, six being sold to Bolivia (*HL*)

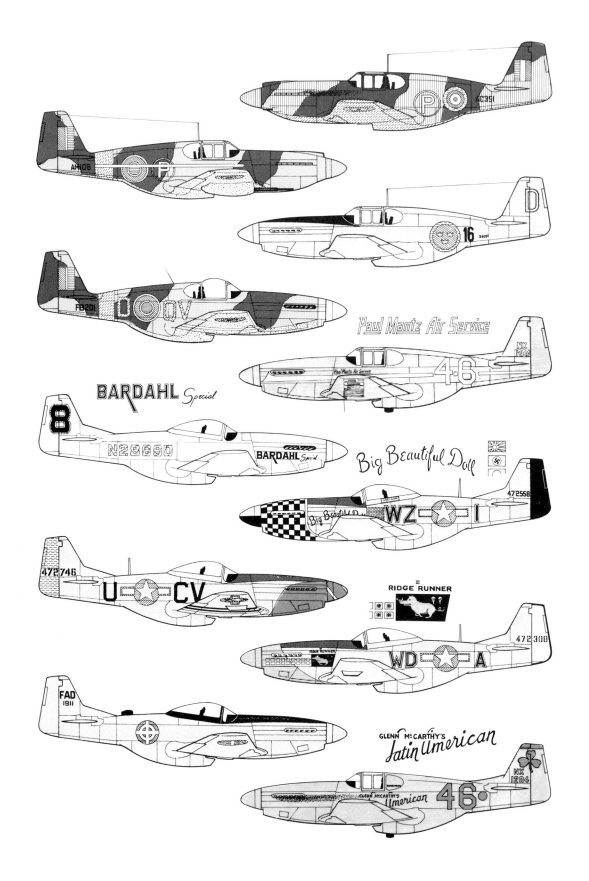

AC351

AM106 P

16 24001 D

FB201 D OV

Paul Mantz Air Service NX 1204 4·6

BARDAHL *Special*

8 N28690 *Bardahl Special*

Big Beautiful Doll 472558 WZ I Big Beautiful D...

472746 U CV

III
RIDGE RUNNER 472308 WD A

FAD 1911

GLENN M^cCARTHY'S *latin American* NX 1204 46· GLENN McCARTHY'S American

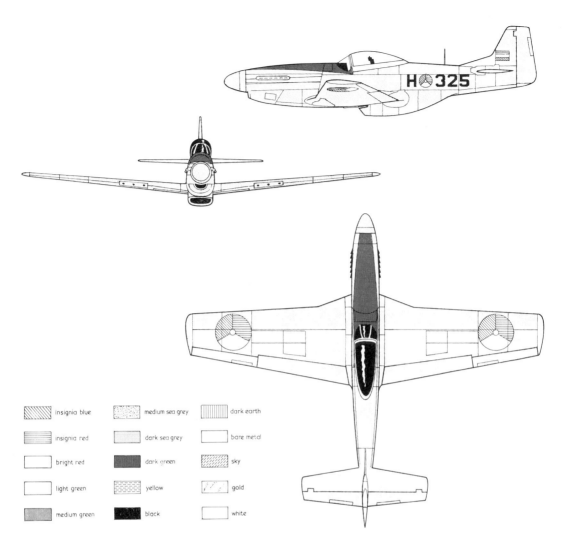

insignia blue	medium sea grey	dark earth
insignia red	dark sea grey	bare metal
bright red	dark green	sky
light green	yellow	gold
medium green	black	white

(*Above*)
P–51D–25–NT H–325: 44–84474 of No 122 Sqn of the Royal Dutch Air Force (Militaire Luchtvaart) as used in the Dutch East Indies; based at Medan, Sumatra, May 1947

(*Left from top to bottom*)
Mustang I AG351 of Air Fighting and Development Unit, Duxford, 1941

Mustang I AM106 with trial installation of two 40mm Vickers 'S' cannon

P–51B–5–NA Mustang 26001 (ex-43–6365 'Z Hub') forced down in Sweden and interned; seen as evaluated by Flygvapnet (the Royal Swedish Air Force)

Mustang III FB201: QV–D of No 19 Sqn, Ford, Sussex in 1944

P–51C–10–NT NX1204 of Paul Mantz, as flown into second place in the 1949 Bendix Trophy by Stan Reaver at 450·221mph; it was the winner in 1948

P–51D N2869D as flown by Charles 'Chuck' Lyford in the 1965 Harrah's Trophy donated by a Reno gambling casino; Merlin engine boosted to an estimated 3,400 hp by Bardahl

P–51D–20–NA 44–72258: WZ–I 'Big Beautiful Doll' flown by Lt Colonel John D. Landers, CO of the 78th Fighter Group, US 8th Air Force; now restored at Duxford, Cambridge

P–51D–25–NA 44–72746: CV–U of Lt Colonel Donald Baccus, CO of 359th Fighter Group, US 8th Air Force

P–51D–20–NA 44–72308: WD–A 'Ridge Runner' of Major Pierce McKennon, CO of 335th Fighter Sqn, 4th Fighter Group, US 8th Air Force at Debden, Essex

P–51D– FAD 1911 of the Dominican Air Force (El Cuerpo de Aviacion Militar Dominicana) Escuadron de Caza; ex-Swedish Air Force J 26

P–51C–10–NT NX1204 'Latin American' as sponsored by Texan oil magnate Glenn McCarthy, for the 1948 Bendix Trophy which it won, flown by Paul Mantz

Displayed outside the Museo de la Revolucion, Havana, this P–51D Mustang flew with the Cuban Fuerza Aérea Rebelde against President Batista's forces. There are dummy bombs under the wings; the serial '401' is in black; the airscrew spinner is yellow; there is a red, white and black diagonal stripe around the fuselage. National marking under the wing tip is a white star on red background with black, white and black horizontal bars each side

Bolivian Air Force P–51Ds FAB 511 and FAB 510 after being refurbished and overhauled by Cavalier Aircraft Corporation; FAB 510 in the foreground is now a two-seater—note slightly different rear canopy shape to that of FAB 511. In 1977 the Bolivian Air Force traded in six of its seven remaining P–51Ds, the seventh being retained for a museum (*HL*)

Behind this AT–6F Texan 44–81974 for the Soviet Air Force can be seen a P–51D destined for the Dutch Government, with proper Militaire Luchtvaart (Military Aviation) markings not yet applied—simply a large Dutch flag on the fuselage and wing tip. Behind it is an RAF Mustang IV in the blue and white roundels and fin flashes used in the Pacific theatre at the end of the war, a USAAF F–6D and another Mustang IV. Another Dutch P–51D can be seen at the top of the photo (RIC)

tion (formerly Trans-Florida Aviation). In the early 1960s Bolivia's air force was at a low ebb as a result of political purges of personnel (the country has had over 180 revolutions since becoming independent of Spain in 1825) and lack of funds for new aircraft. There is an unusual incident to be told from those days. A Lockheed Model 049 Constellation of the US non-scheduled operator Lloyd Airlines was flying over Bolivia en route from Miami to Uruguay on what, it transpired, was a smuggling flight, and an F–51D had been sent up to intercept it. But the Constellation pilot took

a shot at the Mustang through an open cockpit window with his revolver and, it seems, succeeded in forcing it down. The Constellation was impounded by the Bolivian authorities at Santa Cruz de la Sierra on 2 August 1961 on suspicion of smuggling, and Lloyd Airlines ceased operations after this incident.

Indonesian operations

As well as Sweden and France, the Netherlands, Italy and Switzerland all used P–51Ds after the war. Three were acquired by the Royal Dutch Air Force in 1948 for use as ground trainers in Holland, but the Mustang was not used by Netherlands-based fighter squadrons, which had Spitfire 9s as piston-engined equipment after the war. However, forty P–51Ds were delivered to the Dutch Militaire Luchtvaart (or Military Aviation) after the war for use in the East Indies, especially against the Indonesian nationalist forces whom the Dutch had been fighting and against whom they resumed military operations on 19 December 1948 following the rejection by both sides a year before of the proposals of a United Nations committee for the transfer of power from the Dutch to the Indonesians. These operations continued until October 1949, and initially the Mustangs were going to replace the ageing Curtiss P–40 Kittyhawks of No 120 Squadron, forming two new squadrons as well, Nos 121 and 122, in May and November 1946 respectively; in 1949 No 121 was disbanded and its Mustangs went to re-equip No 120 Squadron, whose Kittyhawks had remained in service. A number of P–51K–NT Mustangs—reported to be thirty —were also delivered to the Militaire Luchtvaart, but because of a serious shortage of pilots the Ks were only used to replace P–51Ds that had crashed, been damaged in action or become unserviceable for technical reasons. These were the only P–51Ks to be exported after the war. An interesting in-the-field modification made by the Militaire Luchtvaart was the conversion of two Mustangs into two-seaters similar to the TP–51D, but with the passenger aft of the pilot facing backwards instead of forwards.

After hostilities had ended and the state of Indonesia was officially inaugurated in August 1950, the Militaire Luchtvaart handed over most of its aircraft to the newly formed Indonesian Republic Air Force (Angkatan Udara Republik Indonesia —AURI). The Mustangs formed the back-bone of the AURI's fighter strength, equipping the sole fighter unit, No 3 Squadron, throughout the 1950s and continuing to do so after Russian types, such as MiG jet fighters, largely re-equipped the AURI's combat elements in the 1960s; three new fighter squadrons equipped with MiGs were formed, but the lack of comprehensive spares backing for the Russian types seriously affected operational strength and by 1975 all the Soviet-supplied aircraft acquired under President Soekarno's régime had been grounded. But the Mustangs soldiered on in the fighter-bomber and COIN roles and their numbers, which had dwindled to five P–51Ds in 1973, have since been increased to fourteen by examples acquired from other sources, as part of a modernisation programme of large-scale re-equipment by US and Western combat, training and transport types. The Mustang has been in longer continuous service with Indonesia's air force (now renamed Tentara Nasional Indonesia Angkatan Udara) than with any other air arm and its twenty-eight years of continuous service here is one which few, if any, World War II piston-engined fighters can match. It is now supplemented in the COIN

The Philippine Air Force used a number of P–51Ds until 1959, these equipping one squadron; the one seen here, P–51D–25–NA 44–73007, retains its old USAAF serial and has extra-long drop tanks (AP)

role by sixteen Rockwell International OV–10F Broncos.

A few P–51Ds were supplied to the Philippine Air Force in the 1950s and were used as fighter-bombers, equipping one squadron. They were replaced eventually by some of the forty North American F–86F Sabre jet fighters acquired in 1957–8 which, together with eighteen F–86D Sabres, equipped the 5th Fighter Wing. One other Asian country, South Korea, acquired P–51D Mustangs, a number of these equipping the 10th and 11th Fighter Wings of the Republic of Korea Air Force during the Korean War and serving until they began to be replaced by F–86F and F–86D Sabres supplied under the Military Assistance Programme from 1955. Some of these Mustangs were ex-Royal Australian Air Force P–51Ds that had been supplied to Australia under Lend-Lease and subsequently used in Korea by No 77 Squadron.

Like her fellow neutral Sweden, Switzerland after the war had ordered de Havilland Vampire jets for her air force and decided to acquire surplus USAAF P–51D Mustangs as interim equipment to replace the older piston-engined types. Some 140 P–51Ds were obtained for the Swiss Air Force (or Flug-

The Republic of Korea Air Force used P–51D Mustangs in the early 1950s to equip its 10th and 11th Fighter Wings; some of these were ex-Royal Australian Air Force P–51Ds of No 77 Sqn (*HH*)

waffe, as it was known) from 1948, these replacing the Messerschmitt Bf 109Es that were the mainstay of the Swiss fighter force, the last Bf 109E being withdrawn from service on 28 December 1949. The Mustangs remained in Swiss service for a decade, being finally retired in 1958, and one is now preserved in the Swiss Transport Museum at Lucerne. The Italian Air Force (Aeronautica Militare, as it was then known) also used P–51D Mustangs in the early post-war years; early in 1949 Italy's Minister of Defence gave a detailed break-down of the strength of the Aeronautica Militare, which then had 48 Mustangs, 80 Spitfire 9s and—for reconnaissance—56 Lockheed Lightnings. By 1955 there were still a small number of Mustangs in service but these were finally replaced by Vampire F.B.5s, F–86K Sabres and Republic F–84F and RF–84F jets. A few Italian Air Force P–51Ds were supplied to Somalia's Air Corps (the Cuerpo Aeronautica della Somalia) when it was established as an Italian-controlled force, and since 1963 both Italy and Russia have been supplying aid. The Soviet contribution started with MiG–15 jets, which after a few years replaced the Mustangs in the fighter-bomber role, and has grown considerably in the last few years as the strategic importance of the Horn of Africa to the Kremlin as a means of controlling the Indian Ocean in particular has increased.

From 1951 onwards New Zealand

acquired thirty P–51D Mustangs for its Territorial Air Force which had been set up after the war and flew Oxfords, Harvards and Tiger Moth trainers at first. But the Mustangs were withdrawn from service in 1955 and the Territorial Air Force returned to Harvards as its main equipment until it was disbanded in 1957. One of the RNZAF Mustangs, NZ2417 of No 3 Squadron (previously 45–11507), later came on to the civil register as ZK–CCG

The Swiss Air Force obtained some 140 P–51D Mustangs from 1948; J–2113 seen here is displayed in the Swiss Transport Museum at Lucerne (*JMGG*)

P–51D Mustangs of an Italian Air Force fighter-bomber unit in the field (*HH*)

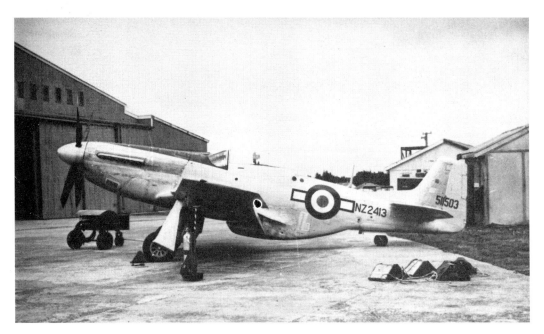

The Royal New Zealand Air Force used thirty
P–51Ds for its Territorial Air Force from 1951
to 1955; seen here is NZ2413 still wearing on the
fin and rudder its old USAAF serial 45–11503 (*HH*)

owned by J. S. McDonald and R. Fechney,
who flew it from Christchurch's Harewood
Airport. The Royal Canadian Air Force,
which had flown Mustangs with the RAF
since the Dieppe raid of August 1942, continued to use P–51Ds after the war, acquir-
ing 30 in 1947 and 100 more in 1950–1; they
equipped some of the ten Auxiliary squadrons that constituted the reserve force, and
for a time the type was also used for tactical
reconnaissance in the RCAF itself.

Mustangs in Korea

Both the Royal Australian Air Force and
the South African Air Force took part in
the Korean conflict with Mustang squadrons; the SAAF had first used Mustang IVs
when its No 5 Squadron re-equipped with
them in Italy as part of the Balkan Air
Force in September 1944. The RAAF's No
77 Squadron with its Mustangs was based at
Iwakuni in Japan, a former naval air
station 450 miles west of Tokyo on the
Inland Sea, as part of the British Commonwealth Occupation Force when the North
Koreans crossed the 38th parallel into South
Korea on 25 June 1950. Directly news of
the invasion was known the US 5th Air
Force was placed on standby and No 77,

which was under its operational control,
was ordered to stand by at 11.00am the
same day. Australia was the first country to
follow President Truman's lead in supporting the South Koreans; on 30 June the
Prime Minister, Mr Robert G. Menzies,
announced in Canberra that No 77 Squadron's services had been offered in Korea.
On 2 July the unit's Mustangs took off
from Iwakuni to escort USAF B–29 Superfortress bombers attacking the North
Korean airfield of Yongpu, near Hamhung,
and on the 7th of that month the first
casualty was sustained when Sqd Ldr G.
Strout failed to pull out of a dive when his
Mustang was attacking Samchok railway
station. On 12 October No 77 moved to
Pohang in South Korea and in the following
month crossed the border with the USAF
35th Fighter Group to a new base at Hamhung, and from there to Pusan. It continued
ground strafing in support of the land forces
and escort work until May 1951 when the
squadron returned to Iwakuni to re-equip
with Gloster Meteor F.8s which it flew until
it returned to Australia in December 1954.

The South African Government offered
to send a fighter squadron to Korea as part
of the United Nations Forces, this unit—
No 2 (Cheetah) Squadron—to be composed
entirely of volunteers, and just over 200
were finally selected. After a spell of battle
training they sailed from Durban on

(Above)
No 2 (Cheetah) Sqn of the South African Air Force used P–51Ds in Korea in the ground attack role and suffered heavy casualties; one of the Squadron's Mustangs taxies out on a Korean airstrip with two bombs and four 5in HVAR rocket projectiles under the wings (*SAAF Official via HH*)

27 September 1950 under the command of Commandant S. Van Breda Theron, DSO, DFC, AFC, and the squadron went to Johnson Air Base near Tokyo for conversion to the F–51D Mustang, of which twenty-five had been bought initially to equip it. On 16 November No 2 moved to K–9 airfield near Pusan which it shared with the USAF's 12th Fighter Squadron as part of the US 18th Fighter-Bomber Wing. The first operational sortie was flown on 19 November, and soon after No 2 moved to K–24 airfield near Pyong-Yang and got its first real taste of the severe Korean winter. In the first wave of the Korean advance, US, British and South Korean forces had been driven into a small perimeter around Pusan out of which they broke on 15 September, capturing Seoul ten days later. By the end of October UN ground forces in their subsequent advance had almost reached the Manchurian border, but Chinese forces had now entered Korea and they counter-attacked on 26 November, driving the UN forces steadily back until the retreat halted at the Imjin river in March 1951.

No 2 made ground strafing and dive-bombing attacks against ground targets in the face of heavy anti-aircraft fire and attacks by MiG–15s and suffered consider-able losses; no less than 58 Mustangs were lost to ground fire, 2 were shot down in air battles and 13 were lost through other causes. The original total of 25 aircraft had been increased by a further 70, replacement Mustangs being flown over from Tokyo. At the end of 1952 No 2 flew its remaining F–51Ds back to Tokyo and began converting to the F–86F Sabre, which the squadron flew in the last few months of the war until the armistice was signed on 27 July 1953. In Korea No 2 had flown a total of 10,373 sorties with Mustangs and 2,032 with Sabres, and 34 out of the 208 pilots who served there did not return to the Union. Altogether 272 decorations were awarded to members of the squadron and in August 1956 it received the rare distinction, for a foreign unit, of being awarded the coveted US Presidential Unit Citation 'for extraordinary heroism in action against the enemy of the United Nations from 28th November 1950 till 30th April 1952'. It is a very different world we live in now:

(Right)
P–51D Mustang 9566: FB–N, one of 130 acquired by the Royal Canadian Air Force after the war. An RCAF Mustang was used by the Canadian National Research Council's Flight Research Establishment to dive-test the wing sections of model supersonic aerofoils in one research programme, and also for experimental work on radar altimeters, magnetometers etc, flying from the NRC's Arnprior airfield near Ottawa.

(Right)
The prototype Cavalier two-seat executive version of the Mustang developed by Trans-Florida Aviation Inc (later Cavalier Aircraft Corp) (*HL*)

today no South African contingent would be acceptable in a UN peacekeeping force, and the UN has shown itself unable to act decisively against Communist aggression.

The executive Mustang

With the Mustang well established on the racing scene and available in larger numbers to civilian buyers than almost all other World War II fighters, it was a logical step to exploit its possibilities as an executive and sporting type for the business or private owner. This was done by Trans-Florida Aviation Inc of Sarasota-Bradenton Airport, Sarasota, Florida, whose president, David B. Lindsay Jr, and his colleagues developed several specialist versions of the F–51D Mustang for the executive and COIN roles. First of these was the Cavalier, a tandem two-seater executive and sporting conversion of the F–51D available in several different variants differing only in their fuel capacity. The Cavalier 2000 was the basic version, with two 110 US gal wingtip fuel tanks bringing the total fuel capacity to 374 US gal which gave a no-reserves range with maximum installed fuel of 2,000 miles; hence the '2000' in the designation, and the suffix number used to differentiate the Cavalier variants was, in fact, this same no-reserves range in miles when fitted with full normal tankage. All variants had provision for two 110 US gal drop tanks under the wings when optional internal wing fuel cells were not installed.

The only Cavalier conversion registered in Europe was I–BILL (ex-P–51D–30–NA 44–74694) owned by the Italian company Billi & Co and based at Florence. It crashed at Mainz, West Germany, on 3 July 1977 killing O. Haydon-Baillie, a noted restorer of World War II vintage aircraft who had just acquired the Cavalier, and his passenger. Note taller fin and rudder similar to the P–51Hs and 110 US gal underwing drop tanks (*JMGG*)

Two people were seated in tandem under the one-piece bubble canopy with the pilot in front in a manner similar to the TP–51D–NT, but more luxuriously, and considering that the Mustang was never designed to take a second occupant the rear seat position was much roomier and gave a better view than might reasonably have been expected. Baggage space was provided behind the rear seat or in the wings, depending on the fuel tankage. The cabin and seats had de luxe ribbed upholstery with foam rubber cushions and floor carpets, and new cabin sound-proofing and insulation were provided, as well as modified heating and ventilation systems installed in the canopy. There were independent demand-type oxygen regulators for pilot and passenger supplied by oxygen bottles in the rear fuselage or, optionally, from a high-pressure oxygen system. The instrument panel was completely redesigned and featured standard blind-flying instrumentation with a variety of optional 'extras'. These included a Sperry H6–B electrical gyro, a Sperry C14 gyrosyn compass system, a Regency 505 transponder, a Collins PN 101 flight director

This is one of several US civil P–51Ds converted into two-seaters using the Cavalier Aircraft conversion kit (HL)

system, Bendix T12C ADF, a Brittain B4 autopilot, Distance Measuring Equipment and a Safe-Flight SC24 speed control system. Radio could be installed in the instrument panel or aft of the passenger's seat, according to customer requirements.

There was a step in each flap to facilitate entry into the cockpit, and the Goodyear wheels had Goodyear multi-disc brakes. The same Packard Merlin V–1650–7 as on the F–51D was fitted, but rated at a higher horsepower of 1,595; it drove a Hamilton Standard 24D50–65 four-blade constant speed airscrew. Trans-Florida Aviation (or rather Cavalier Aircraft Corporation, which it had now become) also marketed two-seat conversion kits for Mustang owners who can do their own Cavalier conversions, and kits were also offered for several other parts of the complete Cavalier conversion, such as wing-tip tanks and internal fuel tanks, modified baggage compartment doors, the modernised Aeroquip fuel system, anti-collision beacons, high-pressure oxygen installations and anti-icing installations.

The prototype Cavalier conversion, registered N551D, first flew in this form in 1961, and a number have since been supplied to executive and private owners in the States; the Cavalier 2000 was being offered at a price of $32,500 in 1961. The Cavalier 750 is the same as the Cavalier 2000 but without the wing-tip tanks, and its total fuel capacity is two 92 US gal tanks in the wing roots. The Cavalier 1200 is the same as the 750, but with two additional L-shaped bladder tanks in the wings of 48 US gal capacity each, bringing total tankage up to 280 gals. The Cavalier 1500 is also the same as the 750 but, instead of L-shaped bladder tanks as in the 1200 it has two rectangular-shaped ones of 63 US gal capacity each, making its total tankage 310 gal. The Cavalier 2500 is basically the same as the 2000, but with two 60 US gal internal wing cells added to the two 92 gal wing-root fuel tanks and the two wing-tip tanks to give a total fuel capacity of 484 US gal.

The COIN Mustangs
The Vietnam war led to a great revival of military interest in specialist COIN or counter-insurgency aircraft for use against guerilla forces such as the Viet Cong who, although not themselves possessing any significant air power or armoured vehicles, could and often did strike back with accurate anti-aircraft fire and sometimes with missiles. For COIN aircraft now sheer speed was less important than the ability to carry a heavy load of high explosives and other weapons, to operate from forward airstrips that would often be short and badly surfaced and to withstand battle damage. Also important were good front-line serviceability and a sturdy undercarriage with low-pressure tyres. Cavalier Aircraft produced a

reworked version of the F–51D for the COIN role in 1967 known as the Mustang II, which made its first flight in December that year; this featured strengthened wings and fuselage structure, a taller fin and rudder and a dorsal fin similar to the P–51H's, modern updated avionics and an ejector seat. Powerplant was a 1,760hp British-built Merlin 620 instead of the Packard Merlin V–1650–7. Underwing hard points provided for the carriage of an external war load of 4,000lb, or twice as much as the wartime P–51B, C and D could carry, but the same fixed armament of six 0·5in Browning machine-guns in the wings was retained. Two 110 US gal wing-tip fuel tanks were fitted, and drop tanks could also replace external 'stores' on the underwing hard points. A two-seat trainer version of the Mustang II was also produced with a second seat behind the pilot similar to the Cavalier executive versions, but with full dual controls. Under USAF contract Cavalier Aircraft then supplied a dozen remanufactured F–51Ds for delivery under the Military Aid Programme to various Latin American countries, and these incorporated most of the features of the Mustang II, such as strengthened wings with eight hard points underneath, the taller fin and rudder similar to the P–51H's, a second seat behind the pilot and Packard Merlin V–1650–7 engines; one was to TF–51D standard with full dual controls. Two similar Cavalier conversions were also purchased by the US Army for use as chase aircraft, these two-seaters being unarmed and having two 110 US gal wing-tip tanks. The Mustang II was superseded by a new turboprop version, the Cavalier Turbo Mustang 3.

A possible turboprop version of the Mustang had in fact been schemed by North American at the end of the war, and an artist's impression of this shows a slim engine nacelle with two contra-rotating airscrews and an exhaust pipe in the port side of the fuselage just over the wing root; the maximum speed of this project would have been over 500mph. The Turbo Mustang 3 was produced as a private venture, and was fitted with a 1,740ehp (maximum take-off) Rolls-Royce RDa.6 Dart 510 turboprop taken from a United Air Lines Viscount 745, which gave 1,490ehp maximum cruising power. There were several good reasons for choosing a turboprop: few countries with pretensions to a modern air force would now choose to re-equip with piston-engined types, especially for combat duties; high-octane aviation fuel, especially in the forward battle areas, constituted a greater fire risk; and the turboprop not only had a higher power-to-weight ratio but was cheaper, more reliable and simpler to maintain than a piston engine of comparable power—a very important consideration for COIN operations. Moreover the Rolls-Royce Dart was in very widespread use, had then 45 million hours of commercial operation behind it, a time between overhauls of 6,000 hours and a low shut-down rate of one per 330,000 hours. It was available in a number of versions up to 3,200shp from

The prototype Cavalier Turbo Mustang 3 seen here has a much slimmer cowling for the Rolls-Royce Dart 510 turboprop, and the ventral radiator scoop is deleted. Six low-drag bombs are carried under the wings, and the tip tanks are of 120 US gallons capacity (*Pilot Press Ltd*)

which a customer could choose to suit his requirements, and Cavalier intended to instal the 2,185shp (maximum cruise power) RDa.7 Dart 529 in the Turbo Mustang later.

The Dart was installed in a slimmer, Viscount 700-type nacelle with the cowling opening out, clamshell fashion, in four main sections for ease of servicing, and the ventral radiator of piston-engined versions was deleted. The exhaust efflux pipe is in the starboard side of the fuselage, over the wing leading edge and just forward of and below the windscreen. This positioning of the exhaust, by shielding the hot gas outlet, helps to give a low infra-red 'signature' on enemy radar screens. The four-blade Dowty-Rotol variable-pitch airscrew—like the engine, the same as on the Viscount—is of 11ft 6in diameter, and propeller pitch and power are both controlled by linkage to a single pilot control that synchronises power settings automatically with the propeller pitch position. The propeller can also, by means of a protected switch, be set in a maximum drag, or flat pitch position to provide controlled deceleration to shorten the landing run. There are two 92 US gal self-sealing fuel tanks in the wing roots and two 120 US gal chord-line wing-tip fuel tanks are fitted as standard; these can increase the loiter time in the target area by up to as much as four hours. Two 110 US gal drop tanks can also be carried on the inner pair of underwing hard points, and an optional extra is the lining of all fuel tanks with reticulated foam for fire suppression.

A number of airframe changes have been made: a taller fin and rudder, similar to the P–51H's, gives improved directional stability, and there is provision for fitting a second seat for a pilot to undergo operational training, the bubble canopy shape being revised slightly to give its occupant more headroom. This revised canopy and second seat have been fitted to several piston-engined F–51Ds refurbished for foreign air forces and to a few US civil-registered ones. Many internal modifications have been made, especially structurally; the rear fuselage has stronger longerons between the cockpit and tail unit, and additional spars and webs have been added to the wing structure to take the six underwing 'stores' hard points. The prototype

had multiple disc brakes and production Turbo Mustangs would have had anti-skid brake units. Other optional extras include a North American LW-3B ejector seat, and structural plastic armour for the engine cowling, cockpit area and wing fuel lines, as well as the reticulated foam lining for fuel tank fire suppression mentioned previously; the customer could specify his own choice of updated avionics.

The inner two underwing hard points can take 1,000lb loads and the four others 750lb each; wing armament, at six 0·5in Browning M2 or M3 machine-guns, remains the same as the wartime versions, and there is a Cavalier Mk 1 illuminated non-computing gunsight. A wide variety of external 'stores' can be carried, including Mk 81 or Mk 82 low-drag 250lb bombs, M–117 or M–64/A1 general-purpose bombs, SUU–11/A 7·62mm machine-gun pods or similar SUU–12/A pods for 0·5in guns, XM–75 grenade launchers, and several different types of rocket launcher: the 19-tube LAU–3A, the 7-tube AERO–6A or the 7-tube LAU–59. Bomblet dispensers or fire bombs can also be carried externally, and for photo reconnaissance a number of strike, horizon-to-horizon, continuous film strip and framing cameras can be fitted. The armament control panels are remounted on the port side of the cockpit coaming, so that the pilot can select his 'stores' without taking his eyes off the target. The production version with Dart 529 could have operated over a 173-mile radius with a maximum armament load of 4,550lb and an over-target capability of $1\frac{3}{4}$ hours, or over a maximum radius of 575 miles with four Mk 81 low-drag 250lb bombs. Basic empty weight was 6,816lb while the maximum gross weight with external stores, at 14,000lb, was just over twice that figure, indicative of the load-carrying capacity the turboprop had made possible. Most spectacular of all, however, was the Turbo Mustang's claimed maximum cruising speed, without any external loads, of 540mph, allied to a take-off run to clear 50ft in sea level, ISA conditions with 2,000lb of armament, of 1,320ft. Although it was demonstrated to USAF Tactical Air Command at Langley Air Force Base, Virginia, and to USAF Systems Command, no production orders were placed.

Based on flight tests of the Turbo Mustang 3, a new COIN version of the F–51D was designed by David B. Lindsay, president of Cavalier Aircraft, and his team; this was similar in all major respects but was powered by a 2,535shp (maximum take-off) Lycoming T55–L–9 shaft turbine. The first of two prototypes, one a single-seater and one a two-seater, first flew on 29 April 1971 and this version's development was taken over by Piper Aircraft Corporation, who named it the Enforcer. Like the Turbo Mustang it had six underwing hard points and wing-tip tanks, as well as the taller fin and rudder; the Lycoming exhaust efflux pipe was on the port side of the fuselage. But after the first prototype Enforcer crashed on 12 July 1971, further develop-

Following tests of the Turbo Mustang 3, a new COIN version was developed by Cavalier powered by a 2,535shp Lycoming T55–L–9 shaft turbine, and development of this was taken over by Piper Aircraft Corporation as the Enforcer, of which the prototype is seen here. Note 120 US gal tip tanks and taller fin and rudder (*Via Air Pic*)

ment was abandoned. The second prototype was one of three aircraft evaluated in the USAF's Pave COIN project of 1971 to select an off-the-shelf specialised tactical aircraft for Forward Air Control duties and light strike missions, and although the Enforcer was not ordered it is a tribute to the basic soundness of this three-decades-old design that it could still be seriously considered for the very different air warfare conditions of the 1970s.

6 The Racing Mustangs

The Mustang had gone through its war service with fewer major modifications than a good many of its contemporaries; of these, the change-over to the Rolls-Royce Merlin and the 'bubble'-type cockpit canopy were the most important. And because it was a comparative latecomer, not seeing action until 1943, it had not been used for so many experimental or research jobs or trial installations of armament and the like as some of its contemporaries, such as the Spitfire or Mosquito. But with the end of the war the Mustang embarked on a new career as a racer, in which role it has now been used in greater numbers and over a longer period—over three decades—than any other fighter, and it is for the racing role that some of the most interesting—and

drastic—modifications to the basic Mustang airframe have been made. Indeed, it is the racing pilots who have between them stretched the Mustang airframe to its limits, quite as much as the North American design team did between 1940 and 1945 to meet the demands of war, and racing modifications have sometimes been every bit as drastic in their redesign and advanced in their technology as any introduced to meet the unexpected needs of war. They have ranged all the way from the by now almost commonplace use of high boost pressures, often with water injection and extra high octane fuels, through 'wet' wings in which the wing itself is sealed to retain fuel, wing leading-edge and wing-tip radiators, cockpit canopies reduced in size or otherwise modified and clipped wings, right through to the installation of a Rolls-Royce Griffon 57 driving a 13ft 8in diameter de Havilland six-blade contra-rotating propeller in Mustang N7715C, flown by Roy ('Mac') McClain. This major modification, sponsored by Red Baron Flying Service of Idaho

The Harrah's Trophy unlimited closed course race at the Los Angeles National Air Races, Fox Field, Lancaster, California on 6 June 1965. From left to right, Clay Lacy in his purple P–51D N182XF, Lyle Shelton in P 51D N66111, E. D. Weiner in Mustang N335 and Darryl Greenamyer in P–38L Lightning N138X (HL)

Falls, and developed at a cost of $350 000, is of a magnitude comparable to the original installation of the Merlin in the Mustang. Yet these high-technology racing modifications have been conceived and executed by a racing pilot and a small team of enthusiasts without any of the massive financial and design resources of a big aircraft company, and their success is all the more impressive because of that. Because there is so little margin for error financially as well as technically, a major racing modification has to be right first time and there can be no question of pouring in thousands of dollars to get a given technical 'fix' right, as might be done by a manufacturer free to pass on the resulting increase in price to his customers.

The first post-war US National Air Races held at Cleveland, Ohio, from 30 August to 2 September 1946 were very different from those of the 1930s, for the specialist racing aircraft of pre-war years had been completely displaced by war-surplus fighters like the Mustang, stripped down by their owner-pilots, with armament and military equipment removed and highly boosted engines. The entire fields for both the prestigious Bendix Trophy race, a speed dash over the 2,048 miles from Van Nuys, California, to Cleveland Municipal Airport, and the Thompson Trophy race, over ten laps of a 30-mile triangular course, consisted of war-surplus fighters, not only Mustangs but also Lockheed P–38J, P–38L and F–5G Lightnings, Bell P–63 Kingcobras and P–39 Airacobras and Goodyear FG–1D

Corsairs. These too, like the Mustangs, were to be subjected to modifications over a period, sometimes drastic ones. Sometimes these mods dictated the shape of the course, as was the case with P–63C–5–BE Kingcobra NX62995 flown by Charles Tucker in the 1946 Thompson Trophy, which had no less than 6½ft cut from each wing tip to reduce the span from the normal 38ft 4in to a mere 25ft. At a pre-race gathering of pilots a three-pylon course was considered, but Tucker said he couldn't hold altitude in his small-span P–63 for more than a 90-degree turn, and so a four-pylon course was decided upon. Tucker was unlucky enough to be out in the first lap as his undercarriage did not retract properly.

For 1946 the Bendix Trophy was divided into reciprocating engined and jet engined sections, and a field of twenty-two surplus fighters lined up at Van Nuys Metropolitan Airport for the former event on 30 August; fourteen of these were P–38 or F–5G Lightnings, and only four Mustangs, so at least one Lightning should have been among the prizewinners. But in fact the Mustangs swept the board, the first three places in the speed dash to Cleveland being taken by converted P–51C–10–NTs and fourth place by a P–51D. The winner was Paul Mantz in his red Mustang NX1202

Miss Jacqueline Cochran's P–51C–10–NT NX28388 as flown in the 1947 Bendix Trophy race by Bruce Gimbel, for which it had two drop tanks. Note slogan 'Air Power Is Peace Power' on the cowling (*HL*)

who covered the course non-stop in 4 hours, 42 minutes and 14 seconds at an average speed of 435·501mph, almost 15mph faster than Miss Jacqueline Cochran, who was second in a time just under ten minutes slower, averaging 420·925mph in her green P–51C NX28388 which had 'Wanted A Strong Coequal Air Force' stencilled under the exhaust pipes, and two big long-range tanks under the wings. Third was Thomas Mayson in P–51C NX1204 (entered by Paul Mantz), taking just a minute over five hours to average 408·220mph and fourth was William Eddy in P–51D NX66851 'City of San Diego', who landed twenty-eight minutes after Mayson having averaged 373·252mph.

Two reasons stood out for Mantz's victory by a sizeable lead over the rest of the field: a mirror-smooth finish to his Mustang and the use of the so-called 'wet' wing in which the wing structure itself was sealed to form the fuel tank and retain fuel. This principle is commonplace today but was still very much a novelty back in 1946 outside the realms of combat aircraft; it had been conceived by Major Alexander P. de Seversky of Republic before the war. Mantz had obtained factory drawings of the Mustang from North American and made exact wing templates for his P–51C; he then spray-painted the low areas to make the wing absolutely smooth and wet-sanded, waxed and polished the entire aircraft to a mirror-smooth finish. He had the fuel filler hose wrapped with dry ice to condense the fuel before taking off, this enabling him to cruise fast all the way, flying at 20,000–30,000ft depending on the winds forecast, and at 33,000ft most of the way for this particular race. Yet all this preparation nearly went for naught when his undercarriage doors closed before the wheels had retracted after take-off, but Mantz put the Mustang into a tight loop, which opened the doors and enabled the gear to be retracted properly. This was his fourth attempt at the Bendix Trophy; he had come fifth in the 1935 contest and taken third place in both 1938 and 1939. He now had the satisfaction of beating the 1938 winner, Jacqueline Cochran, into second place in the first post-war contest; the big external tanks on her Mustang created extra drag, emphasising the advantage of a 'wet' wing.

The other major event, the Thompson Trophy, was a closed-circuit race over ten laps of a 30-mile course around four pylons, this type of race providing more spectator appeal than the long speed dash of the Bendix Trophy, as the whole of the race could be flown within sight of the watching crowds. Like the Bendix, the Thompson Trophy was now divided into jet and piston-engined sections, and pylon racing in much more powerful World War II fighters heightened the twin problems of overtaking and propeller wash that had always been there, but were given new emphasis by the speed and horsepower of the aircraft involved. Rules on passing were that pilots had to fly 150ft to the right or 50ft above, and they were warned about trying to pass underneath unless their competitor had sufficient height, and also about giving sufficient clearance at the pylon to the plane on their left, and not crowding him. Prop wash and the aircraft's wake were also a problem, as they could flip a close-following aircraft into an uncontrollable high-speed roll from which, at such a low altitude, there could be no escape.

Winner of the 1946 Thompson Trophy, flown on 2 September, was Bell test pilot Alvin 'Tex' Johnston in a stripped-down P–39Q–10–BE Airacobra NX92848 'Cobra II' at 373·9mph, with Lockheed test pilot Tony Le Vier second in his bright red P–38L–5–LO Lightning NX21764. Third, fourth, fifth and seventh places were taken by P–51D Mustangs flown by (respectively) Earl Ortman (in NX66453), Bruce Raymond (in NX79111), Robert Swanson (in NX79161) and Woodrow Edmundson (in NX69406). Ortman averaged 367·625 mph and George Welch in P–51D NX37492 was hot on the tail of the winner, Johnston, until he had to retire in the second lap with engine trouble. P–51D Mustangs also took first two places in the Sohio (or Standard Oil Co of Ohio) Trophy for aircraft unable to qualify for the Thompson Trophy; this took place on 31 August over eight laps of a 30-mile triangular course. First was Dale Fulton in NX33685 and second was William Ong in NX61151. A big change from pre-war years was that the Thompson Trophy pilots wore G suits to enable them to make high g turns without blacking out, and most of them also used oxygen masks to avoid

asphyxiation from leaking fuel or exhaust fumes. An important difference between British and American air racing was the lack of a handicapping system in the States, and the US preference for a massed 'race-horse' type of start for races such as the Thompson Trophy, while several races just for one type of aircraft evolved to meet the needs of lower performance types such as T–6 Texans which would not have stood a chance in the big unhandicapped events.

The first US post-war Nationals had been a success, and for the 1947 National Air Races, the record total of some 3,500 private aircraft flew into Cleveland during August 30–September 1, over 2,500 of them being parked on the airport—the largest gathering of private owner types ever seen. The piston-engined section of the Bendix Trophy, flown on 30 August over the same course as 1946, from Van Nuys to Cleveland, attracted a smaller field of twelve entries; half of these were Mustangs and they took the first six places. Paul Mantz was the winner for the second year in succession in his red and white P–51C–10–NT NX1202, taking only 4 hours, 26 minutes, 57 seconds over the 2,048-mile course to set a record average speed of no less than 460·423mph. Only 78 seconds behind him in P–51D NX33699 'Magic Town' was Joe C. DeBona, who averaged 458·203mph; both the first two arrived in a

Earl Ortman's P–51D NX66453 came third in the 1946 Thompson Trophy, and was one of the first to have clipped wings, 18in being cropped from each wing tip (*HL*)

rainstorm that cancelled all other race events for the day. Mindful of Mantz's 1946 success, DeBona had had his black and white Mustang modified to have a 'wet' wing and, like Mantz, flew at full throttle and high altitude the whole way. Third was Edmund Lunken in P–51D NX61151 'Buttonpuss', who took 43 seconds over 5 hours with fuel stops, and averaged 408·723 mph, followed by Bruce Gimbel in Miss Jacqueline Cochran's P–51C NX28388, who averaged 404·080mph; fifth was William Eddy in P–51D NX66851 'City of San Diego', at an average speed of 376·549mph, and sixth was Thomas Mayson in P–51C NX1204 who averaged 376·084mph.

But it was the 1947 Thompson Trophy that was to be the most spectacular and casualty-strewn in the race's twelve-year history; out of a field of 13, 4 aircraft crashed, 3 more retired and only 6 finished the 20-lap course over 300 miles. Only 12 aircraft had actually qualified; the thirteenth, Curtiss XP–40Q Warhawk NX300B, was flown by Joe Ziegler who took off in the confusion at the start. His engine failed just after passing pylon 4 in the fourteenth lap, and he bailed out, breaking a leg; the XP–40Q's falling cockpit canopy injured a

Second in the 1947 Bendix Trophy was
Joe DeBona in his black and white P–51D–10–NA
NX33699 'Magic Town', which featured a 'wet'
wing like the winner, Paul Mantz's P–51C–10–NT
NX1202 (*HL*)

Edmund Lunken's P–51D NX61151 'Buttonpuss'
as it appeared in the 1947 Bendix Trophy with
standard canopy, finishing third (*HL*)

woman and a wing tore the top off a boxcar
in a nearby railway siding, and then
exploded on striking the ground between
two boxcars, damaging the tracks. The
XP–40Q, of which only one was built, was
the penultimate version of the Warhawk.
But the first casualty had been P–51C
Mustang NX4814N, which suffered engine
failure as it passed the home pylon just
after the start; the pilot, Jack Hardwick,

belly-landed but tore a wing off and escaped from the burning P–51 with only a bruised elbow. The next to drop out was Charles Walling in P–38J Lightning NX25Y, who landed with mechanical trouble in the second lap. Next casualty was Paul Penrose in P–51D Mustang NX37492, who force-landed successfully after engine failure in the sixth lap, while in the next lap Tony Jannazo was killed instantly when he lost control of his big Goodyear F2G–1 Corsair and flew into the ground near pylon 2 at around 400mph. The torque stick forces from the F2G–1's big four-bladed propeller were very high in turns, especially tight pylon turns, and required both hands on the stick to overcome them; this may well have been why Jannazo crashed.

While rounding pylon 3 on the eleventh lap, the Allison V–1710 of Woody Edmundson's P–51A NX4E exploded and he crash-landed; he was taken seriously injured from the burning wreckage but later recovered. The Mustang was also repaired, and was one of the very few Allison-powered ones used in post-war racing. Another F2G–1 flown by Ron Puckett force-landed successfully after engine failure in the nineteenth lap, and the final winner was Cook Cleland in F2G–1 Corsair NX5577N who established a six-mile lead at the finish and averaged 396·131mph; the F2G–1's 28-cylinder four-row Pratt & Whitney R–4360–4 Wasp Major radial engine was the biggest piston engine ever to be used in US air racing, and developed over 4,000hp. Cleland had mortgaged himself to the hilt in buying and modifying three surplus F2G–1s for racing, but his victory in the 1947 Thompson Trophy brought him $19,500 prize money. One of his F2G–1s flown by Richard Becker took second place, third place went to Jay Demming in a P–39Q–10–BE Airacobra and fourth was Steve Beville in P–51D Mustang NX79111.

A new event for 1947 was the Kendall Oil Trophy race for Mustangs, which attracted a field of seven, two of which retired. Jack Hardwick in P–51C NX4814N, who later crashed in the Thompson Trophy, was forced out in the third lap and Anson Johnson in P–51D NX13Y retired in the fifth lap. The winner was Steve Beville in P–51D NX79111 at an average speed of

384·602mph; second was Kendall Everson in an A–36A Mustang (the only one of this version used for racing) at an average of 377·926mph, followed by Woody Edmundson, third, in P–51A NX4E, then M. W. Fairbrother, fourth, in P–51D NX65453, and finally William Murray in P–51D NX66851. From 1948 the Kendall Trophy was made a ladies' race for women AT–6 Texan pilots.

The 1948 Nationals were again held at Cleveland, during 4–6 September, and the Bendix Trophy, flown this year from Long Beach, California, to Cleveland (a distance only three miles shorter than the previous year) was notable for the closest finish in its history, the first three pilots, all flying Mustangs, arriving within eighty seconds of each other. The field was much smaller —only six aircraft—reflecting, perhaps, the expense of racing fighters with powerful and fuel-hungry engines and the off-putting effect of the 1947 Thompson Trophy accidents. Winner for the third time was Paul Mantz, who became the only man ever to win the Bendix Trophy three times; this time he flew his light green P–51C–10–NT NX1204, which had come third in the 1946 Bendix flown by Thomas Mayson. Mantz covered the 2,045-mile course in 4 hours, 33 minutes, 48·7 seconds at an average of 447·980mph, and again used dry ice to condense his fuel supply and guard against fuel shortage. Second was Linton Carney in the 1946 and 1947 Bendix winner P–51C N1202, owned by Paul Mantz, which finished just 68·8 seconds behind the latter to average 446·112mph. This was now named 'Houstonian' and painted light green, indicative of its sponsorship by Texan oil tycoon Glenn McCarthy; it also had the racing number '60' previously applied to NX1204, while the latter now carried NX1202's former race number '46'. Third was Jacqueline Cochran in her P–51C NX28388, who averaged 445·847mph to arrive just under 10 seconds after Linton Carney, and fourth was Ed Lunken in P–51D N61151 at an average of 441·594 mph. As 'Buttonpuss' this Mustang had come third in the 1947 Bendix; it now had a smaller cockpit canopy that had been cut down and reduced in height over the standard P–51D canopy, and also featured a 'wet' wing. It also carried the name 'Texan'

Ed Lunken's P–51D 'Buttonpuss' as it appeared in the 1948 Bendix Trophy with a smaller, cut-down canopy and a 'wet' wing; it was now light green all over and also carried the name 'Texan', indicating its sponsorship by Texan oil magnate Glenn McCarthy (*HL*)

on the fuselage and was painted light green to indicate its sponsorship, like NX1202, by oil tycoon Glenn McCarthy. Fifth and last place was taken by Mosquito B.25 N66313, flown by Jesse F. Stallings, president of the then new charter or supplemental airline Capitol Airways Inc, who arrived after just 25 seconds under 6 hours with a dead engine, having averaged only 341·120mph. Joe DeBona, flying F–6C Mustang N5528N, landed out of fuel at Elyria, Ohio, almost in sight of Cleveland. First place in the Tinnerman Trophy Race of seven laps over a 15-mile course went to Bruce Raymond in P–51D NX79111, who averaged 362·245 mph; the rest of the field consisted of three Bell P–63 Kingcobras (one of which retired) and P–51D NX65453 flown by M. W. Fairbrother, which was forced out in the sixth lap. Mustangs also took third, fourth and fifth places in the 1948 Sohio Trophy, which was a restricted and handicap event that year won by Bob Euker in P–63A Kingcobra N69901. Charles Walling in P–51D NX37492 was third, followed by Bruce Raymond in P–51D NX79111 and Charles Bing in P–51A NX4E, which had crashed in the previous year's Thompson Trophy.

That year's casualties were not reproduced in the 1948 Thompson Trophy, held on 6 September, but there were an unusually high number of retirements, seven of the ten starters dropping out at various points in the 20-lap, 300-mile race, but all landed safely. Leading the field until the penultimate lap was 24-year-old war ace Charles Brown in Bell P–39Q–10–BE Airacobra N92848 'Cobra II' which had won this race in 1946. But his engine began cutting out and he was forced to land within a few seconds of victory—all the more disappointing because he had taken one lap at 413·097mph and might well have set a new speed record, having averaged 392·407mph until his retirement. The winner was 28-year-old airline pilot Anson Johnson in P–51D Mustang NX13Y, who averaged 383·767mph and was surprised to win, as he did not know that Brown in the Airacobra and Cook Cleland, the previous year's winner in his F2G–1 Corsair had had to retire. Johnson's dark blue P–51D was almost standard except for a high-gloss wax finish and, with his win making him some $17,000 richer in cash prizes, he recalled after the race that in the previous year, after coming unplaced in the Kendall Trophy, he had had to borrow five dollars to get out of town.

Second was Bruce Raymond in P–51D NX79111, who averaged 365·234mph, and third was Wilson Newhall in P–63C–5–BE Kingcobra NX69702 at an average of 313·567mph. Among those who retired were M. W. Fairbrother in P–51D NX65453, out in the thirteenth lap, Woody Edmundson

in P–51A NX4E, out in the fourteenth and Charles Walling in P–51D NX37492 who dropped out in the eighteenth lap. Most competitors used 145 octane fuel and water injection systems for extra power.

An interesting Mustang that failed to qualify for the 1948 Nationals was P–51D N68183 'Connie III', flown by James DeSanto, which featured wings clipped by 2½ft each side, almost the first time clipped wings had appeared on a racing Mustang. DeSanto 'blew' his V–1650–3 Merlin engine on his qualifying flight when increasing his boost pressure to 100 inches of mercury. This was DeSanto's third try at the Nationals and he had had little luck; he only took sixth out of seven places in the 1946 Sohio Trophy because the spark plugs on the port engine of his Lockheed F–5D Lightning NX49721 'Connie I' fouled, and for the 1947 Nationals he bought the sole example of the big Curtiss XP–60E fighter, selling his flying school to raise the money. This was much modified by Curtiss for racing, with wings clipped by 10ft 2in to a span of 31ft 2in and the Pratt & Whitney R–2800–10 Double Wasp engine 'souped up' to give 2,440hp and 90 inches of mercury boost with water injection. It was registered NX21979 and named 'Connie II', but on a test flight just before qualifying for the 1947 Nationals it suffered a failure of the tail surfaces and DeSanto bailed out, landing safely.

The 1949 National Air Races were held during 3–5 September at Cleveland, and this year the Bendix Trophy was over a slightly shorter course, covering 2,008 miles from Rosamond Dry Lake in California to Cleveland. As the year before, there were only six entries and the first three home were all Mustangs, the winner being Joe DeBona in F–6C N5528N at a record average speed of 470·136mph, taking 4 hours, 16 minutes, 17 seconds. For this year's contest, and mindful of how he had landed short of fuel so near to Cleveland in 1948, because of headwinds, DeBona had modified his Mustang to have a 'wet' wing, like the P–51D NX33699 'Magic Town' in which he had come second in 1947. Second was Stan Reaver in the 1948 winner, P–51C N1204, which had reverted to its original red and white colour scheme; he averaged 450·221 mph and took 4 hours, 33 minutes, 17 seconds. Third was Lockheed test pilot Herman 'Fish' Salmon in the 1946 and '47 winner, P–51C N1202, who took 4 hours, 28 minutes and 13 seconds to average 449·214mph. Fourth was Don Bussart in de Havilland Mosquito B.25 N37878, 'The Wooden Wonder', who suffered engine trouble five minutes after take-off and flew virtually all the way with his starboard airscrew feathered and out of oxygen to average only 343·757mph. Lee H. Cameron, flying Martin B–26C Marauder N5546N 'Valley Turtle', fitted with extra fuel tankage in the bomb bay, had to land at North Platte, Nebraska, for fuel line repairs and

Joe DeBona's F–6C Mustang N5528N, in which he won the 1949 Bendix Trophy at the record speed of 470·136mph, also featured a 'wet' wing (*HL*)

arrived at Cleveland after the deadline, while another type that was even more of an outsider, Republic AT–12 Guardsman advanced trainer NX55811, named 'Buck Rogers' and flown by Vincent Perron and featuring a 'wet' wing, was forced to retire at Grand Junction, Colorado. For the first time that year a 'racehorse'-type start had been used for the Bendix Trophy. The Tinnerman Trophy Race was won by Ben McKillen in Goodyear F2G–1 Corsair N5588N at an average speed of 386·069 mph, with Wilson V. Newhall second in P–51K Mustang N40055 at an average of 379·735mph; third was Fl Lt J. H. G. McArthur RCAF in Spitfire F.R.XIVE CF–GMZ at 359·565mph—the only Spitfire to race in the US Nationals. Of the six remaining aircraft entered, James Hannon in P–51A Mustang NX39502 was out in the seventh lap and Anson Johnson in P–51D N13Y did not start.

With three years' post-war racing experience behind them, pilots were now attempting more drastic modifications to their aircraft, and two variations on the radiator theme were of especial interest, the wing leading edge radiators of Anson Johnson's P–51D N13Y and the wing-tip radiators of P–51C Mustang N4845N 'Beguine', owned by Jacqueline Cochran and flown by Captain Bill Odom; in both cases these replaced the conventional ventral radiators.

Bill Odom had already established himself as the most famous US post-war civilian pilot by dint of his round-the-world solo record flight of 73 hours, 5 minutes, 11 seconds in August 1947 in the Douglas B–26 Invader 'Reynolds Bombshell', and another solo flight, this time non-stop, of 5,000 miles between Honolulu, Hawaii and New Jersey in a Beech Bonanza which set a new world class distance record for light planes. Odom's Mustang 'Beguine' had the radiators mounted in two nacelles on the wing tips in a very neat installation carried out by Garrett AiResearch with North American engineers also working on the P–51C as an outside project; 20–30 inches of each wing tip and aileron were removed to accommodate the radiator, and the reduced wing area and end-plate effect of the radiator pods reduced drag considerably, while the radiator heat added thrust. But this was at the price of reducing aileron span and therefore effectiveness considerably, with unfortunate results that were to be seen in the Thompson Trophy. A brand new Packard Merlin V–1650 with accessories was installed, modified to run at 3,400rpm and driving a special 'one off' Hamilton Standard paddle-bladed propeller with extremely thin section blades especially made for wartime tests at North American, this resulting in a speed increase of about 12mph.

'Beguine' was finished in an attractive dark green colour scheme with the musical notation of Cole Porter's hit number 'Begin the Beguine' stencilled right down the fuse-

lage and on the radiator pods. After achieving 405·565mph in his qualifying flight, with the throttle not fully open, Odom entered the Sohio Trophy to gain pylon racing experience and gained an easy first place at an average speed of 388·393mph, beating eight other contestants; Steve Beville in P–51D NX79111 was fourth at 376·719mph, Ken Cooley in P–51D N37492 was fifth and M. W. Fairbrother in P–51D N65453 took seventh place. In this race Odom was saving his engine for the big event, the Thompson Trophy, but it was obvious that 'Beguine' was very fast.

The other major radiator modification, to Anson Johnson's P–51D N13Y (ex–44–

Captain Bill Odom's ill-fated P–51C Mustang N4845N 'Beguine' was modified by Garrett AiResearch for the 1949 Thompson Trophy to have wing-tip radiators and a special Hamilton Standard airscrew with very thin section blades. But during a steep turn Odom got into a high-speed stall, flipped over on to his back and crashed; the weight of the radiator pods and the reduced aileron span had made the stick forces too great for recovery at such low altitudes (*HL*)

Odom's P–51C, actually owned by Jacqueline Cochran, had the music of Cole Porter's number 'Begin the Beguine' stencilled right down the fuselage and on the radiator pods (*HL*)

72400), took the form of Bell P–39 type radiators and their intakes in the wing and its leading edges, occupying the space where the gun bays had been; the radiator shutters were located just ahead of the flaps, resembling small air brakes when opened, the radiator efflux exhausting over the flaps. Repainted yellow with red lettering for the 1949 Thompson Trophy, engine trouble prevented the P–51D from realising the full low drag potential of the new radiators; Johnson found his undercarriage would only partially retract through the first lap and, having corrected this, he found that the exhaust pipes were starting to burn off and the Merlin was throwing off a substantial amount of oil, even though the oil temperature and pressure gauges were reading correctly. Rather than risk an engine failure and crash, Johnson retired in the ninth lap. Cook Cleland, the 1947 Thompson winner, had also modified his big F2G–1 Corsair N5590N, fitting a hydrogen peroxide injection system to the Wasp Major engine, enabling over 4,000hp to be developed at a boost pressure of 65 inches of mercury—low indeed for racing. The wing tips had been clipped 18 inches each for the 1948 race and were cropped by a further 29 inches this year, bringing the span down to only 33ft 2in, and end plates were fitted to improve handling qualities and reduce tip losses; an airscrew spinner was another innovation. All the entrants for this year's race used water injection systems and 130–170 octane fuels for higher power.

Ten entrants—three F2G–1 Corsairs, six Mustangs and a Bell P–63C Kingcobra—took off in a 'racehorse' start at 4·40pm on 5 September for the Thompson Trophy, which this year was 15 laps over a course totalling 225 miles. All flew below 200ft for the first lap and, entering the second lap, Ben McKillan led the field in his F2G–1 Corsair, followed by Cook Cleland and then by Bill Odom in P–51C 'Beguine'. Then tragedy struck: Odom overturned pylon 2, did a steep turn to the right to try and get back on course but went into a high-speed stall and flipped over on to his back out of control. The aircraft crashed into a house and exploded, killing himself and a mother and her thirteen-month-old boy inside the house. The aileron span and hence effectiveness had been reduced by

the radiator pods of 'Beguine', and the pods' weight—perhaps 200lb each with coolant—increased the aircraft's rolling inertia and raised stick forces in a steep, fast turn to critically high values—so high, in fact, that Odom could not possibly have recovered at such a low altitude as he was flying. The race continued, however, and this time the first three places were taken by the F2G–1 Corsairs, Cook Cleland being the winner at 397·071mph, followed by Ron Puckett, second, at 393·527mph and Ben McKillan third at 387·589mph. Fourth was Steve Beville in P–51D Mustang NX79111 at 381·214mph, fifth was Charles Tucker in P–63C–5–BE Kingcobra N63231, followed by James Hagerstrom, sixth, in P–51D N37492, then Wilson Newhall in P–51K N40055 and finally James Hannon in P–51A NX39502.

The end of the Nationals?

In June 1950 the Korean War broke out and no National Air Races were held that year; some racing pilots went back to active service, including Cook Cleland, the 1947 and 49 Thompson Trophy winner and an experienced Navy pilot with a distinguished war record, who returned to active service as a lieutenant-commander and CO of a carrier-based Corsair squadron, VF–653, off Korea in February 1951. The 1951 National Air Races were held, not at Cleveland, but at Detroit, Michigan, on 18 and 19 August and this year neither the Bendix nor the Thompson Trophy piston-engined divisions were run, but only the jet sections. As a result, that year's Nationals were dominated by the military, Colonel Keith Compton in an F–86A Sabre flying the 1,919·6 miles from Muroc Dry Lake in California to Detroit in only 3 hours, 27 minutes, 56 seconds at a new record speed of 553·8mph to win the Bendix Jet Trophy. Second was Colonel Emmett Davis in an F–84E Thunderjet, who averaged 534·9mph, and third and fourth places were taken by two North American B–45C Tornado jet bombers. The field for the Thompson Jet Trophy was even smaller, there being only one entry—Colonel Fred Ascani in an F–86E Sabre who set a new record speed for the race of 628·698mph over the one-lap 62·14-mile (100-kilometre) course. Two days before, Colonel Ascani had set a world record of 635·411mph over the same course, breaking John Derry's record speed over a 100km closed circuit of 605·2mph set up on 12 April 1948 in the de Havilland DH 108. The General Electric Trophy and Allison Trophy were two other jet fighter races, and the only civilian contest in 1951 was sponsored by Continental Motors and was for the Formula 1 midget racers.

These were to be the last Nationals in their early post-war form, for a number of reasons. Bill Odom's crash in the 1949 Thompson Trophy, and the casualty-strewn race of two years before, had begun to raise doubts about the safety aspects of racing fast and powerful fighters around pylons at very low altitudes, while in the jet sections of the Bendix and Thompson Trophies the Air Force and Navy had been barred from competing against each other since 1948 by the Secretary of Defense, and after the 1949 Thompson Jet Trophy, the USAF had decreed that there would be no more pylon racing between their aircraft. So the inter-Service competition that could have provided so much spectacle in air racing was barred, and there was also the point that the number of entries had got smaller for the Bendix Trophy piston-engined section

from 1946 to 1949, although not so much for the Thompson race. And, except for the midget racers, the Nationals were becoming increasingly hard to justify as a source of technological improvement in areas such as fuels or aero engines, which might be used for the betterment of future designs, and which these races undoubtedly were in the 1920s and 1930s. But now it was military/government research budgets that were more likely to be the major source of technical innovation, and racing modifications like the 'wet' wing introduced by Paul Mantz were more likely to have had precedents in military use. The Thompson Trophy had been instituted in 1930 by the late Charles E. Thompson, a noted Cleveland manufacturer of car and aircraft valves, to stimulate the development of faster aircraft at a time when the United States seemed to be lagging behind Europe in the quest for speed, but by the 1950s it was the Americans who were drawing further and further ahead of Europe with types such as the Bell X–1 and F–86 Sabre.

So the Nationals ended with the 1951 contests, and for the next nine years (except for 1953, when there were no races) air racing in the States was confined to the midget racers under various sponsors, chief among them Continental Motors, and it was to be another thirteen years before racing in the States was revived on the scale it had enjoyed in 1946–9. Meanwhile, some

Johnson's Mustang as modified for the 1949 Thompson Trophy with Bell P–39 type radiators in the wing with leading edge intakes; repainted yellow with red lettering, engine trouble forced it to retire in the ninth lap (*HL*)

notable record flights were made by Captain Charles F. Blair in the 1946 and '47 Bendix Trophy winning P–51C–10–NT Mustang N1202 which he had acquired from Paul Mantz. Renamed 'Excalibur III' and retaining the 'wet' wing (its total internal fuel capacity was no less than 865gal), this was flown by Captain Blair between New York and London on 31 January 1951 to set an unofficial solo record for the eastbound crossing in a time of 7 hours, 48 minutes between Idlewild Airport and London Heathrow at an average speed of 442mph. As a senior Pan American skipper who by 1969 had amassed some 34,000 flying hours and 1,400 Atlantic crossings, Captain Blair was very familiar with this route. On 30 May 1951 he made an even more notable flight in 'Excalibur III'—the first solo flight across the North Pole. Taking off from Bardufoss in Norway, he landed at Fairbanks, Alaska, 10 hours 29 minutes later after covering a distance of 3,375 miles; this was by far the longest non-stop flight ever to be made by a Mustang, and Blair later flew 'Excalibur III' on to New York. This Mustang was eventually presented to the Smithsonian Institute in Washington, DC. Captain Blair, who also held the rank of Brigadier-General in the USAF Reserve and acted as a navigation consultant to the USAF and NASA, subsequently led the first flights (with flight refuelling) of USAF F–100 Super Sabres to cross the North Pole (this was called 'Operation Julius Caesar'), and the first transatlantic flights of Republic F–84 Thunderjets to England ('Operation Shark Bait'). Late in 1963 he formed a flying boat airline, Antilles Air Boats, to operate services with Grumman Goose amphibians between St Thomas and St Croix in the US Virgin Islands. The airline in 1968 went on to operate a Vought-Sikorsky VS–44A and from 1974 a pair of Short Sandringham flying boats.

Reno revival

From 1961 to 1963 there were no air races at all in the States, even for the Formula 1 midget racers, which had continued with a few small events sponsored by racing pilots' associations after Continental Motors had withdrawn its backing in 1952. But in the winter of 1963–4 a group of racing enthusiasts headed by the late Bill Stead, a rancher-pilot of Reno, Nevada, who was better known as a hydroplane racer, laid ambitious plans for a revival of air racing on the old Cleveland scale. It was to cover the whole spectrum from unlimited class cross-country and closed course races for piston-engined types corresponding to the old Bendix and Thompson Trophies, down to Formula 1 races, pylon races for home-built single-seat biplanes and a ladies' race flown in Piper Cherokees. Additional attractions were ballooning, aerobatics, soaring and parachuting, so there was even more spectacle than in the old days at Cleveland, and the only things lacking were high-speed military jets. But, contrary to what many people must have expected, it proved to be possible to stage air racing on this scale without the backing of either the military or big companies such as Bendix, Goodyear or Sohio who had sponsored the Cleveland races, and prizes were put up by the local community and outside interests. That for the Transcontinental Trophy Dash was sponsored by a Reno gambling casino known as Harold's Club, and the site for the 1964 revival of air racing, held during 12–20 September, was a makeshift one at Sky Ranch, north of Reno, later to be replaced from 1966 by the former Stead Air Force Base which had much better runway and hangar facilities, and clearly visible courses for the closed circuit events.

By 1964 Mustangs were still plentiful; the USAF had put up 100 for sale in 1957 alone, and the Royal Canadian Air Force, and several other air arms, had disposed of their Mustangs as surplus at around this time; so that by 1965 there were no less than 202 on the US civil register, of which 87 were still active, many of these being used for racing and others as Cavalier executive versions. By contrast, most of the other fighters against which Mustangs had raced at Cleveland in the early post-war years, such as the P–39 Airacobra and P–63 Kingcobra, the Corsair and the P–38 Lightning, had by 1964 mostly disappeared into museums or other static displays, although a P–38L did make a solitary reappearance in the 1965 races. So races from 1964 were even more dominated by Mustangs than they had been at Cleveland, and had it not been for the Grumman F8F–2 Bearcats and (from 1966) the Hawker Sea Fury to add a bit of variety, the races might have suffered somewhat as a result as a spectacle for the lay public.

All eight entrants for the first Harold's Club Trophy Dash, held on 12 September over the 2,254 miles from St Petersburg, Florida, to Reno, were P–51D Mustangs, the race finishing in front of the grandstand during the meeting. The winner was Wayne Adams in P–51D N332, who took 7 hours, 4 minutes, 7 seconds to average 318·88mph; his chocolate-brown Mustang, which made one refuelling stop, featured a 'wet' wing giving it an internal fuel capacity of 600 US gal. Second was Charles Lyford in N2869D, who arrived just over 15 minutes after Adams, having averaged 307·78mph, and third was C. E. Crosby in ex-RCAF P–51D N35N 'Mr Choppers', whose three fuel stops lengthened his time to 8 hours, 8 minutes and 27 seconds; his average speed was 276·92mph. Fourth was Dick Snyder in N651D 'Phoebe II' (an ex-RCAF P–51D), followed by Jack Shaver in Cavalier N351D, who burst his tyres landing at Oklahoma City and, last, Stan Hoke in Cavalier N551D. Two other competitors made landings in Florida because of bad weather and did not complete the course; E. D. 'Ed' Weiner in N335J landed at Jacksonville and Howard Olsen in N5073K put down at Ocala. Times and speeds were noticeably slower than in the post-war Bendix races over a course of similar length, owing to bad weather and headwinds, which caused Stan Hoke, the last man, to lose two hours refuelling at a USAF base when weather prevented his planned Albuquerque stop.

Five P–51D Mustangs and three Grumman F8F–2 Bearcats qualified for the unlimited class closed course race for Harrah's Trophy, and because the dirt runway at Sky Ranch was too narrow for a 'racehorse' start the four preliminary heats and the final race were made from flying starts. The race was ten laps over a course totalling 80·19 miles, and points were awarded for each heat. The winner was Bob Love in P–51D N2869D, which had a very 'souped up' Packard V–1650–7 Merlin modified by the Bardahl team of race specialists under Ron Musson to deliver an estimated 3,400hp at a boost pressure of 110 inches of mercury. Love had qualified at a speed of 395·46mph and achieved 405

mph in one heat, but throttled back to win the final race at only 366·82mph. But, having cut two pylons in one of the heats, he was second on points to Mira Slovak in F8F–2 Bearcat N9885C, who was sponsored by Smirnoff Vodka and who had come second in the finals at 355·52mph, but was the victor on points. Third was Clay Lacy in P–51D N182XF at an average of 354·74mph, fourth on points was Ben Hall in P–51D N5482V 'Seattle Miss', followed by Commander Walter Ohlrich, fifth, in F8F–2 Bearcat N7827C, and sixth, E. D. Weiner in P–51D N335J. Darryl Greenamyer, a Lockheed test pilot on the SR–71 and YF–12, was placed fourth in the finals in F8F–2 Bearcat N1111L, but was disqualified for failing to land back at the race site. Instead Greenamyer had landed on the wide runways of Reno Municipal Airport, largely because the visibility from his cut-down cockpit canopy was too poor for a safe landing on the Sky Ranch runway.

The nine-day revival of racing at Reno had attracted over 100,000 spectators and was sufficiently successful to prompt several other places to stage air races in 1965; there were midget racer and homebuilt biplane contests at St Petersburg, Florida, more midget racing at Palm Springs, California, and unlimited class, biplane and midget racing at Las Vegas and Los Angeles as well as Reno, both the Los Angeles and Reno contests being held at Fox Field, Lancaster, California. The Los Angeles National Air Races were scheduled for 29–31 May at Fox Field, but owing to high winds over the Mojave Desert the final day's events were postponed for a week until 6 June. That day the unlimited class closed course race was held over 15 laps totalling 135 miles, the field being five P–51D Mustangs, Mira Slovak in his Bearcat and Darryl Greenamyer, this time in a bright red P–38L Lightning N138X 'Yippee' as his Bearcat was being modified. Dave Allender in P–51D N5452V dropped out just after take-off with a high coolant temperature reading which turned out to be false, and a unique starting method was used, the six remaining pilots forming themselves into line abreast by radio control, and then flying over the starting line at a few hundred feet while the starter's flag went down. Ben

A well-known competitor in most of the unlimited class races since the 1964 revival at Reno was Clay Lacy in his purple P–51D N182XF, popularly known as the 'Purple People Eater' and later registered N64CL (*HL*)

One of E. D. Weiner's two P–51Ds, N335 had a 'wet' wing and a cut-down cockpit canopy, and sported a striking black and white checkerboard fuselage, fin and rudder (*HL*)

Hall in P–51D N5482V 'Seattle Miss', with a Merlin modified by the well-known Bardahl team, had to retire hurriedly in the sixth lap when a connecting rod bolt broke, causing the crankshaft to break and resulting in major damage to the engine; Hall just managed to get down on the runway. The winner was Charles 'Chuck' Lyford in the much-boosted P–51D N2869D in which Bob Love had won at Reno the previous year; Lyford's speed, even though he throttled back a bit on the last two laps,

was still 390·61mph. Clay Lacy in P–51D N182XF, also with a 'souped up' Merlin, was second at 370·54mph, having nearly lost this place to Mira Slovak in the Bearcat when he eased back a bit in the thirteenth lap and Slovak slipped under him, but Slovak was beaten into third place by just three seconds, averaging 369·64mph. Fourth was Darryl Greenamyer in the P–38L Lightning and fifth E. D. Weiner in P–51D N335, a 'wet' wing Mustang with the fuselage, fin and rudder painted in a striking black and white checkerboard colour scheme.

From 1965 onwards, the National Championship Air Races were held at Reno every September as the premier event in the racing calendar, the Nevada gambling capital having now replaced Cleveland as the centre of air racing in the States. There were nine entries for the Harold's Club Transcontinental Trophy over the 2,260 miles from St Petersburg, Florida, to Reno and all were P–51D Mustangs except for a Riley Rocket (modified Cessna 310) which retired with engine trouble, as did Jim Fugate's P–51D N5077K. Winner was E. D. Weiner in P–51D N335 at an average speed of 348·6mph, a slowish speed which reflected a 10-minute stop at Duncan, Oklahoma, to take on 400gal of fuel; this P–51D had a 25gal water-methanol tank behind the pilot's seat for use on take-offs. Second was Clay Lacy in P–51D N182XF at 342·4mph and third was Wayne Adams, the 1964 winner, in P–51D N332. Seven P–51D Mustangs and three F8F–2 Bearcats qualified for this year's unlimited closed course race for Harrah's Trophy, sponsored by another Reno gambling casino. Even so, the first prize was a mere $2,000, which would about pay for an engine overhaul, compared with the $19,500 earned by Cook Cleland when he won the 1947 Thompson Trophy. The 1965 winner was Darryl Greenamyer in his Bearcat at a slowish 375·10mph—pilots were not going to burn up their engines for such small prize money—and Charles 'Chuck' Lyford was second at 368·57mph in P–51D N2869D; third was Clay Lacy in P–51D N182XF, the race consisting of ten laps of an eight-mile course. Only a fortnight after this race on 26 September, most of the same pilots were lining up for the start of another unlimited closed course contest for

the Paul Mantz Trophy, part of the Las Vegas International Air Races at Boulder City Airport, Nevada. As at Reno, there were two heat races before qualifying, and after pulling out of the second heat with a 'blown' engine, Bob Abrams in his P–51D crashed and was killed through turning too tightly into his final approach. Three P–51Ds and three Bearcats qualified for the finals, Darryl Greenamyer in his F8F–2 doing so at a record speed of 423·40mph, with 'Chuck' Lyford in his P–51D N2869D not far behind at 418·14mph. In the race, there was a neck-and-neck duel between these two for the first six of the ten laps of 9·35 miles each, but Greenamyer began to slow in the seventh lap and finally had to drop out in the ninth with mechanical trouble. Lyford was the winner at an average of 391·62mph, followed by Ben Hall, second, in P–51D N5482V and Mira Slovak third in his Bearcat N9855C. Clay Lacy in his purple-coloured N182XF was penalised for cutting two pylons; this Mustang, like most of the unlimited racers, had a water-methanol injection system.

The Reno revival of 1964 had clearly been no flash in the pan, and from 1966 a basic pattern now emerged in which the National Championship Air Races were held at Reno in September as the premier event, and two or three other American cities staged major racing events. Between them these covered the whole spectrum from unlimited class to Formula 1, and racing could now be enjoyed by a wider public as it was not concentrated at one city as it had been at Cleveland, while for the pilots the more contests there were the greater their chances of winning some prize money to cover the expense of racing an aircraft like a Mustang. By 1969 at Reno the total prize money available for the winners of five events was no less than $80,000, with $35,850 for the winner of the unlimited closed course event. But it was not always like this: at the 1967 Cleveland National Air Races (the first to be held there for eighteen years) no unlimited cross-country race was scheduled because there was no prize money available. However, E. D. Weiner talked three other unlimited class pilots into putting $1,000 each into a pool for a race over the 1,961·2 miles between Palm Springs, California, to

Cleveland, the winner to take all. Weiner himself won, covering the course on 3 September in five hours at an average speed of some 400mph in his P–51D N335; second was Mike Carroll in Hawker Sea Fury F.B.11 N878M at some 375mph, this aircraft now featuring a 'wet' wing, and Bob Guilford in P–51D N511D came third. Weiner had also won the unlimited closed course race prize money and $5,000 at the 1966 Los Angeles National Air Races held at Fox Field on 30 May; flying his other P–51D, N335J, he averaged 375·18mph, with Ben Hall second in P–51D N5482V and Russell Schleech third in P–51D N332. Darryl Greenamyer had considerably modified and stripped down his F8F–2 Bearcat N1111L for this event and a subsequent attempt on the world piston-engined speed record set up on 26 April 1939 by the Messerschmitt Me 209V1 flown by Fritz Wendel at 469·220mph; he finally broke this record on 16 August 1969 at a speed of 483·041mph. Among his 1966 modifications were cropped wing tips and a fin and rudder shortened by 18in, but the latter gave him inadequate rudder control at high speed for pylon racing. The expression 'hot ship' really meant just that for Greenamyer, whose very 'souped up' non-standard Pratt & Whitney R–2800–34W Double Wasp radial ran so hot that he had to wear Alaskan mukluks to prevent his feet from blistering and a glove on his throttle hand for the same reason; the throttle was much taped to dissipate some heat and, once it was set, he would let go of it!

For the 1966 National Championships, this year held at Stead Air Force Base, Reno, 'Chuck' Lyford's P–51D N2869D was also more drastically modified than before; its wings were clipped by 3½ft and modified Hoerner wing tips were fitted, reducing the span to 30ft. The tailplane tips were also clipped, and wing surfaces were carefully filled in at butt joints, the whole being given a high gloss finish. The Merlin engine was highly tuned and boosted to deliver no less than 3,600hp, more than twice the power of the standard production V–1650–7, and to absorb this power an oversize propeller was fitted, so large that it necessitated three-point landings and take-offs. Mike Carroll's Sea Fury F.B.11 N878M, appearing for the first time that year, was also modified, with 6½ft off each wing and a much smaller cockpit canopy; flown by Lyle Shelton, it was dropped from the finals for mistakenly cutting a pylon during the qualifying heat. 'Chuck' Lyford landed after qualifying at 390·081mph with his white Mustang covered with black oil, and it was found that a connecting rod bolt had snapped and pieces of the rod had torn a hole in each side of the engine block. The damaged engine was replaced with another Merlin for the finals, and the crowd began to hope that they would see the long-awaited duel between Lyford and Greenamyer's Bearcat. The latter and five P–51Ds took off on 24 September and this year were started from the air by test pilot Bob Hoover in his yellow Mustang, who directed the six pilots into line abreast formation by radio, giving the signal to go as all six roared past the stands; this was to become an often-used method of starting. But Lyford was again unlucky; his new engine began to stream oil and smoke and he pulled out in the fifth lap. The water injection system had failed and the resulting 'knocking' had burned a hole through the engine side. Greenamyer was the winner at an average of 396·221mph, with Ben Hall second in P–51D N9885C at 372·701 mph, and Clay Lacy third in P–51D N182XF.

For the 1967 National Championships at Reno, the unlimited closed course race of 10 laps totalling 80·04 miles produced a final field of 6, consisting of Darryl Greenamyer's Bearcat and 5 P–51Ds, all the latter with greatly 'souped up' engines delivering over 2,500hp. E. D. Weiner's P–51D N335J had been modified this year in a way similar to 'Chuck' Lyford's, with the wing clipped to 30ft span with Hoerner tips added, the tailplane also clipped, and a high gloss overall finish with skin butt joints filled in and smoothed; renamed 'Hi Time II', N335J was repainted in a striking zebra-style black and white colour scheme for the fuselage, with white wings and tailplane. After an air start by Bob Hoover in his P–51D on 23 September, the six finalists roared off but Lyford, who had qualified at 400·332mph, was again unlucky; when he was trying to overtake Greenamyer in the first lap at very high speed, oil and smoke started to pour from his engine and he pulled out to make an excellent dead-stick landing on the runway; he had practised such landings often in case of an engine failure. The race was again won by Greenamyer, who averaged 392·621mph, with E. D. Weiner in his zebra-style P–51D second at 373·712mph and Clay Lacy in his purple Mustang third; last was Mike Loening in Ben Hall's former P–51D N5482V, this year renamed 'Chance III' and fitted with a cut-down cockpit canopy. The original canopy was later restored and the wings clipped.

It was not always mechanical or engine failure that caused sudden retirement; at the 1969 National Championships at Reno on 19 September, in the third lap of Heat 1 of the unlimited closed course race, E. D. 'Ed' Weiner flying his checkerboard P–51D N335J suffered a heart attack but succeeded in landing safely after circling the course until all the others had landed. He was rushed to a Reno hospital where, ten days later, he died of heart failure. In an unusual and moving ceremony on 12 October, his ashes were scattered into the Pacific off the California coast from his Mustang N335J flown by Clay Lacy, and five other racing pilot friends of his flew in formation with this P–51D on a last memorial flight; there were Walter Ohlrich and Howard Keefe in Texans, Lyle Shelton in Ed's other 'wet' wing P–51D, N335, now with a cut-down cockpit canopy and painted red over all,

Leroy Penhall in his P–51D N65190 and Roy Berry in Cosmic Wind N20C 'Little Toni'; there was a vacant place in the formation for Ed himself, in recognition of his great contribution to unlimited class racing. Another racing pilot who it is thought may have suffered a heart attack in the air was Dick Kestle, winner of the Harold's Club Transcontinental Trophy in 1969 and 1970, whose P–51D N6303T, en route from Washington Dulles International Airport to Columbus, Georgia, on 4 June 1972 was seen to dive almost vertically into the ground forty miles north of Atlanta in clear weather.

But racing continued to attract plenty of newcomers to take the place of the older hands, such as Bill Hogan, who flew one of the few P–51H Mustangs used for racing, N313H, in an attractive brown, orange and cream colour scheme, and Dr Clifford D. Cummins of Riverside, California, a physician and radiologist who raced the veteran P–51D N79111 now named 'Miss Candace', which first competed in the 1946 Thompson Trophy as the 'Galloping Ghost', and flew in several other races in 1947, 1948 and

P–51D NX79111 'The Galloping Ghost' was flown in a number of races during 1946–9 by Bruce Raymond and Steve Beville; it resumed racing in 1969 in the hands of physician and radiologist Dr Clifford Cummins as 'Miss Candace', and was later fitted with a cut-down canopy and clipped wings (HL)

1949. Having visited Reno several times in this P–51D, Dr Cummins made his debut in racing by coming fourth in the 1969 Harrah's Unlimited Championship race over a closed course (12 laps of 8½ miles) held on 21 September at Reno. The winner was again Darryl Greenamyer in his F8F–2 Bearcat at an average of 412·631mph—a new speed record—and second was airline captain Charles R. 'Chuck' Hall in the very sleek P–51D N7715C 'Miss R. J.' at 377·234 mph. This had clipped wings with modified Hoerner tips to give a span of 30ft, a very clean cut-down cockpit canopy, a longer, pointed spinner and a much-boosted Merlin. A connecting rod broke in the qualifying heat at over 120 inches of mercury boost pressure, but Hall landed safely and, after a team of mechanics had replaced the damaged Merlin with a stock engine, he was allowed to compete even though he had not qualified. Third was Clay Lacy in his purple P–51D N182XF.

In the Harold Club's Transcontinental Trophy from Milwaukee to Reno, Dick Kestle, the winner, carried a navigator in his P–51D N6303T, which was a two-seater

Los Angeles newspaper executive Howard (Howie) Keefe's brightly painted two-seat P–51D N991R 'Miss America' has several non-standard features, such as Hoerner wing tips, a 'souped up' V–1650–9 Merlin and inflatable 50-gal wing bag tanks devised by Keefe himself to fit in the gun bays (HL)

conversion by Cavalier Aircraft, but for the 1970 race which he also won he replaced the second seat with a 90gal fuel tank to bring his total tankage up to 400gal; this P–51D, now named 'Royal Crown Cola', also had a taller P–51H type fin and rudder. Charles P. Doyle took off for this race in his P–51D N711UP from Milwaukee Municipal Airport with a cracked canopy, which failed over Nevada when half the plexiglass came out, but he flew into Reno at reduced throttle to take fifth place; this P–51D also had clipped wings. Another two-seater P–51D in this race was Los Angeles newspaper executive Howard Keefe's N991R 'Miss America' with Pete Hoyt as navigator; they only finished fourth because 125mph headwinds necessitated a refuelling stop. This Mustang, which had a Merlin V–1650–9 developing over 2,000hp, finished fourth in the Harrah's Trophy unlimited championship over 12 laps of an 8·389-mile course, but Keefe nearly lost control entering the tenth lap when his hydraulically-actuated Micarta rudder trim tab malfunctioned and jammed hard over at 450 mph; the P–51D went into a violent right skid towards the grandstands but Keefe reduced throttle and regained control, and it was later found that one half of the tab had blown away and the remaining piece was jammed at a right angle to the rudder.

Keefe developed an interesting modification for his own and other Mustangs in the

shape of inflatable 50gal wing tanks to fit in the gun bays which, when the vents are closed, can be drained completely flat. John Sliker's P–51D N10607 sported another variation in extra tankage in the form of Cessna 310 wing-tip tanks, as well as the Keefe gun-bay tanks, to fly non-stop in the Harold's Club Transcontinental race, in which he was third; he replaced these with fibreglass wing tips for the Harrah's Trophy pylon races and refitted the Cessna 310 tanks for the California 1,000 Mile Air Race; the conventional P–51D tips can also be fitted. Winner of the Harrah's Trophy and $7,200 prize money was Clay Lacy in his purple P–51D, now re-registered N64CL, at 387·342mph, and he won after competing in all ten unlimited class races since 1964; this Mustang's V–1650–9 Merlin drives an Aeroproducts propeller and there is a 33 gal anti-detonation fluid tank in one wing used in conjunction with a plain water tank of the same size in the other wing.

An unusual attempt to combine the merits of both closed course and transcontinental races was the California 1,000 Mile Air Race held at Mojave Airport, Mojave, California on 15 November 1970. Staged over 66 laps of a 15·15-mile course with 10 pylons, it attracted a record field of 20 aircraft. They were ten P–51D Mustangs and one P–51H, one F8F–1 Bearcat and one F8F–2, two Sea Fury F.B. 11s, an F4U–4 Corsair and an F4U–7, a P–38L Lightning, a Douglas B–26C Invader and—most

Another brightly painted P–51D is Kenneth Burnstine's N69QF, with its red and yellow checkerboard tail unit, red, black and white trim and a white star with blue disc on the white cross behind the canopy. This Mustang was fitted with a radiator spray bar to assist cooling in the California Air Classic races at Mojave (*HL*)

unexpected of all—a four-engined ex-American Airlines Douglas DC–7BF airliner, N759Z, named 'Super Snoopy'. This was flown by Clay Lacy, president of the Professional Race Pilots Association as well as being a Super DC–8 captain with United Airlines, with Allen Paulson of California Airmotive, one of the sponsors of Lacy's P–51D, as co-pilot, and it was entered to gain publicity for the event and air racing in general; in this it succeeded, attracting full TV and newspaper coverage, and it finally finished sixth, at an average of 275·87mph. The DC–7BF had been used as a freighter by Zantop Air Transport of Detroit, which later became Universal Airlines Inc, and was acquired by California Airmotive in 1968. With so many laps to be flown, pit stops as in car racing were allowed, the pits being off to the right and inside the main runway; after a pit stop an aircraft would take off inside the race-course on a narrow runway paralleling the main one. Leroy Penhall's P–51D was in the lead until the middle of the race when he pit-stopped at lap 40, and Sherman Cooper went into the lead in the 'wet' wing Sea Fury N878M to win the race and $13,800

Bob Love's P–51D N576GF had several modifications for the 1973 Nationals; the wing and tailplane tips were clipped and a modified cockpit canopy previously used by Dr Clifford Cummins on his P–51D N79111 fitted; this Mustang previously bore the racing number '9' (*HL*)

prize money at an average speed of 344·08 mph, taking 2 hours, 52 minutes and 38 seconds. Second was Dr Clifford Cummins in the 'wet' wing P–51D N332 that had won the first Harold's Club Transcontinental race in 1964 flown by Wayne Adams; this Mustang carried 570gal fuel and had 45 minutes' worth remaining on landing. Third was Mike Loening in his clipped-wing P–51D N5482V.

Modifications continued to be made to Mustangs and other racing fighters, but, curiously enough, the winning speeds set up in the Bendix Trophy during 1946–9 by Paul Mantz and others remained unbeaten by quite a large margin and, as Clay Lacy remarked after qualifying in the unlimited class in 1972: 'It doesn't really seem that the modified Mustangs are doing any better than the Stockers'. Two examples of this in particular had been Charles Lyford's P–51D N2869D and the much modified P–51D N7715C 'Miss R. J.', and another was Dr Clifford Cummins' N79111 'Miss Candace'. This had been fitted with a cut-down cockpit canopy and clipped wings with Hoerner tips for the 1970 Harrah's Trophy race, but was damaged in a dead-stick belly landing in one of the heats. The

radiator intake was damaged and Cummins decided on a rebuild with the radiator intakes in the wing root leading edges, along the lines of Anson Johnson's P–51D in the 1949 Thompson Trophy. Instead, for the 1972 Nationals at Reno, he retained the ventral intake but made it smaller, and the Merlin V–1650–9 engine had different reduction gearing to drive an F8F–2 Bearcat propeller. Acting on bad advice, he qualified at too slow a speed to make the finals, but won the Unlimited Medallion race (for aircraft that failed to make the finals or the Silver Consolation race) easily at 367·564mph. Charles 'Chuck' Hall had sold the P–51D N7715C 'Miss R. J.', with which he had had some disappointments, in July 1971 to machinery manufacturer Gunther Balz. Balz had previously raced a Bearcat, and for 1972 certain airframe changes were made that were reckoned to add 15mph to the top speed, while the Merlin had been modified by Hovey Machine Products of Oakland to give 2,750 hp at 130 inches of boost pressure; it drove an Aeroproducts lightweight propeller and the tailplane had also been cropped. During his heat race on 15 September, in which he had qualified at 395·590mph, Balz lost a sizeable piece of fibreglass skin behind the canopy, but after about 35 hours' work by the ground crew the P–51D was ready for the finals. After the usual air start by Bob Hoover in his P–51D, Balz went on to take the lead from Dick Laidley's Bearcat

(*Above*)
Previously owned by airline pilot Charles 'Chuck' Hall, this much modified P–51D N7715C had clipped wings with Hoerner tips, a longer, pointed spinner and a cut-down cockpit canopy. It was sold to Gunther Balz of the Roto-Finish Co and, with a clipped tailplane and an Aeroproducts lightweight prop, Balz set a new world closed-course record of 416·160mph at Reno in 1972 (*HL*)

(*Below*)
N7715C is seen here in its original re-engined form with a broad-chord fin and ventral under-fin; the latter was later removed and the main fin replaced by one more like the standard P–51D's (*HL*)

in the fifth lap and was flagged down as the winner of the 8-lap race over a 9·815-mile course by 1,500yd over Laidley. He had set a new world closed-course record for piston-engined aircraft at 416·160mph, doing one lap at 430mph and exceeding 460mph on the longest legs of the course; he took $12,500 in prize money—way behind the post-war Thompson Trophy first prizes. Certainly, compared to sports like golf and tennis, air racing's financial rewards, even in the States, are miniscule in comparison to the expenses. The Balz closed-course record was broken at the Nationals a year later both by Lyle Shelton in his Bearcat, the winner at 428·155mph, and Dr Clifford Cummins, second, in his P–51D 'Miss Candace' at 417·076mph.

Yet in spite of the still rather meagre prize-money rewards, racing pilots, to their credit, have again and again embarked on ambitious modifications as if they could expect the financial earnings of an Arnold Palmer or a Jimmy Connors from racing. A prime example of this has been the P–51D N7715C 'Miss R. J.', much modified for 'Chuck' Hall and further modified for Gunther Balz. For the 1975 season this appeared with about the most drastic modification ever made to an unlimited class aircraft—a new engine in the shape of an extensively modified Rolls-Royce Griffon 57 driving a de Havilland six-blade contra-rotating propeller of 13ft 8in diameter. This engine change had been carried out for Roy 'Mac' Maclain by the P–51D's sponsors, Red Baron Flying Services of Idaho Falls, Idaho, a fixed base operator (to use the American regulatory term) which provides charter services, flying training, aerial application such as crop spraying, maintenance and various sales services, mostly in the state of Idaho. The Griffon 57 had been taken from an Avro Shackleton maritime reconnaissance bomber, in which it developed 2,455bhp for take-off, and the 'chin'-type radiator of the Shackleton installation was, of course, replaced by the Mustang's ventral radiator; the carburettor air intake was repositioned on top of the cowling as in the Allison-engined versions. Initially, a fin of much increased chord was fitted, together with a ventral under-fin, but the latter was later removed and the broad-chord fin replaced by one more like the standard P–51D's. Roy Maclain had started racing T–6 Texans in 1972 when a Cessna distributor trading as Mac's Flying Service at Eufala, Alabama, winning the AT–6 Championship Race at Reno that year, and in 1973 entered the unlimited class as well, flying Jack Sliker's P–51D N10607. In 1974 he won the third annual California Air Classic unlimited class race in N7715C before its engine change. Red Baron Flying Services also sponsored Darryl Greenamyer's Lockheed Starfighter, modified for an attempt on the world's low-level speed record and redesignated RB–104.

Winning the King's Cup

In 1967 the Mustang appeared on the British air racing scene when Charles Masefield, flying P–51D N6356T, won the coveted King's Cup at Tollerton, Northamptonshire, at a speed of 277·5mph, the fastest winning speed so far, although slow by us standards; the race was over 6 laps of a 12·5-mile quadrilateral course and Masefield was among 17 entrants. But although, oddly enough, the Mustang did not qualify for entry under the rules of the race, Masefield was not disqualified and his victory has apparently gone unchallenged. The King's Cup rules state that entry is restricted to aircraft registered in or built in the United Kingdom or British Commonwealth and to pilots and entrants of British nationality; Masefield, in good faith, had apparently told the officials that his P–51D had been built in Canada, but this was incorrect as no Mustangs were built in that country. This P–51D was built in the States as 44–74494A and in December 1950 was disposed of to the Royal Canadian Air Force with the serial 9237; in February 1959 it was sold off to the first of several us owners with the us registration N6356T, and the nominal owner at the time of the 1967 King's Cup was an American, Benjamin B. Peck. It had been delivered to the Luxembourg charter airline Interocean Airways SA via Keflavik and Prestwick on 28 July 1964, and two years later went to the British Historic Aircraft Museum at Biggin Hill, being acquired by Keegan Aviation Ltd in January 1967; Masefield did not actually buy it from Keegan until February 1969. In the previous month 20th Century Fox Film Corpor-

For the 1975 Nationals N7715C was modified yet again by the installation of a Rolls-Royce Griffon 57 driving a de Havilland six-blade contra-rotating propeller of 13ft 8in diameter.

This job was carried out for Roy 'Mac' Maclain by Red Baron Flying Services of Idaho Falls, Idaho; on the wheel fairing is the name of Randy Scoville, crew chief (*HL*)

The standard P–51D N6356T in which Charles Masefield won the 1967 King's Cup at Tollerton; colour scheme is red and white (*JMGG*)

ation had bought it from Mr Peck, and a year later it flew four hours in film making. In 1970 it went to Edgar A. Jurist of the Confederate Air Force in Texas.

Masefield won several other races in this Mustang: the Air League Trophy in 1967, the Manx Air Derby in 1968 and the Geoffrey de Havilland Memorial Trophy for the second year in succession. Being handicapped in British races against other light aircraft, Masefield recalled that he started so long after everyone else that he didn't know, literally until the last thirty seconds, whether he was going to finish first or last. During the two years he flew it, he gave over 100 aerobatic displays in the Mustang to cover the cost of running it, which worked out at £50 per hour. Also worth mentioning is the P–51B Mustang that a Frenchman, M Lejeune, intended to base on the South Pacific island of Tahiti; it was allotted the provisional registration F–AZAG in May 1975, but in the end never came on to the French civil register, as M Lejeune's plans fell through.

7 The Twin Mustang

By the summer of 1943 it was clear that a new type of escort fighter would be needed to accompany the B–24 Liberators and also the new Boeing B–29 Superfortress bombers about to enter service in the Pacific theatre, on very long-range raids, without impairing the pilot's ability to fight enemy aircraft when the target area was reached. A consequence of the exceptional range of the P–51 Mustang was that it had made possible escort flights of perhaps six or seven hours, at the end of which time the pilot's reflexes, reactions and judgement in combat had to be as good as the enemy fighters who had just taken off from their bases, and whose pilots were not fatigued by the strain of a long flight. Operations by the USAAF in the Pacific had already shown that single-seater fighter pilots were being subjected to severe strain by the length of typical missions, and a two-man crew was an obvious answer to this problem. Although two-seat versions of the single-engined Mustang such as the TP–51D had been produced, one or two of them 'in the field', the second seat in these occupied the space taken up by the 85gal fuel tank, and so would have sacrificed some of the fuel capacity necessary for very long missions.

So the idea arose of a twin fuselage version of the Mustang in which two P–51H fuselages were joined by a constant chord centre section and a similar tailplane and elevator, the outer wings being basically standard P–51H units. This approach enabled a very useful two-seat long-range escort fighter to be produced much more quickly than starting a new design from scratch; it would have the added safety and reliability of two engines, it could be put into production with the minimum of delay using many existing Mustang jigs and tooling, and use of the P–51's already proven systems would minimise development time and the risk of unexpected snags. The USAAF liked North American's proposals for a twin-fuselage Mustang, and four prototypes of the XP–82, as the new fighter was designated, were ordered on 7 January 1944. The Twin Mustang was, in fact, to be the only twin-fuselage version of a single-engined wartime Allied military aircraft to

go into production in any numbers. The Germans, however, had something of a weakness for this concept, their best known example in this field being the Heinkel He 111Z Zwilling, evolved as a tug for large troop-carrying gliders such as the Messerschmitt Me 321 Gigant. This consisted of two Heinkel He 111H–6 bombers joined together by a common centre section outboard of a port and starboard engine, on which was mounted a fifth Junkers Jumo 211F–2 powerplant. Several German designs were projected in twin-fuselage versions, perhaps the most outlandish of these being the Dornier Do 635, a twin-fuselage version of the Do 335 fighter which had a DB603 engine in front and one in the rear of each fuselage; the Do 635 would have been a four-engined fighter with an engine 'at each corner'.

The first of two XP–82–NA Twin Mustang prototypes made its first flight at Los Angeles on 15 April 1945, some sixteen months after work had started on the project. These two were powered by 1,380hp (maximum take-off) Packard Merlin V–1650–23 and 25 engines driving opposite-rotating airscrews 'handed' to turn inwards towards each other; the pilot was in the port cockpit and the co-pilot in the starboard. Only the port cockpit had the full range of flight and engine instrumentation, the co-pilot having duplicated controls and enough instrumentation for emergency and relief operation of the aircraft. For use in the fighter-bomber or ground attack role the starboard cockpit could be removed and replaced by a metal fairing, thus converting the P–82 into a single-seater, and a proposed interceptor version also had the co-pilot's cockpit canopy removed and the cockpit faired over to save weight and reduce drag; this would have had only internal fuel and no external 'stores'. The rudder pedals in either fuselage could be disconnected and stowed, and there was an automatic pilot in the port cockpit in the F–82E to F–82H versions, with manual emergency release in the starboard one.

The outer wing panels were structurally modified by the deletion of the main wheel well and the three 0·5in Browning machine-

The second prototype XP–82–NA Twin Mustang with Packard Merlin V–1650–23 and 25 engines driving 'handed' airscrews (*RIC*)

guns usually fitted; two 'stores' pylons were fitted under each outer wing with provision for 310 US gal drop tanks or 1,000lb bombs. The centre section was similar in construction to the outer wings with a single slotted trailing edge flap over its full span; it was here that the armament of six 0·5in Browning MG 53–2 machine-guns was relocated, there being a gun bay between the centre-section spars, and the guns fired between the airscrew discs. Two 1,000lb bombs could be carried under the centre section and one under each outer wing, or a 450 US gal drop tank or two 2,000lb bombs could be carried under the centre

The XP–82 Twin Mustang here seen carrying the jettisonable gun pod for eight 0·5in machine-guns under the centre section, with two clusters of five 5in HVAR rocket-projectiles and two 1,000lb bombs under the outer wings (*RIC*)

section; bombs were released electrically from the port cockpit, and could be jettisoned in an emergency by the co-pilot. Five 5in HVAR rocket projectiles could be carried in a cluster under a rack under the centre section, with two more similar racks under each outer wing. A streamlined jettisonable gun pod housing eight 0·5in machine-guns with 400 rounds per gun and carried under the centre section was also developed for the P–82B. Each aileron moved in two sections to allow for wing deflection, there being a controllable trim tab in the inner portion of the starboard aileron. The tailplane and elevator were likewise constant in chord, there being no outer tailplanes, and the tailplane span to the centre-line of each fin was 14ft 4in; the elevator had a controllable trim tab. The basic fins and rudders were the same as the P–51H's, although the dorsal fins were larger.

The fuselages were similar in construction to that of the P–51H, but modified to have an extra section 4ft 9in long inserted aft of the radiator fairing and ahead of the tailplane. Each main undercarriage unit, pivoted on the main spar of the outer wing, at the wing root, retracted hydraulically across the bottom of each fuselage, the wheels going into wells in the centre section. Undercarriage track was 16ft 8¾in, and in the event of hydraulic failure the gear could be lowered by emergency mechanical means. Twin retractable tailwheels, one to each fuselage, were cable-operated from the main gear. Both tailwheels were steered by the rudder bar, or could be disengaged to swivel freely when the control column was pushed forward. Internal fuel capacity was 576 US gal in four self-sealing fuel tanks in the outer wings.

The third prototype Twin Mustang was the XP–82A, powered by two 1,500hp (maximum take-off) Allison V–1710–119 engines that did not drive contra-rotating airscrews like those of the XP–82, but both North American and the USAAF preferred the Packard Merlin, and so this first XP–82A was not completed, the fourth prototype, which was also to have been an XP–82A, being cancelled.

First production version was the P–82B–NA, of which the USAAF had ordered 500 only a few months after ordering the prototypes, and this reverted to the Packard

Merlin, being powered by 1,380hp (maximum take-off) V–1650–9 and 21 engines driving 'handed' airscrews. The first B models began to come off the Los Angeles production line in the spring of 1945, but with the big cutbacks in military orders after VJ Day all but twenty P–82Bs were cancelled. Those built did not go into squadron service but were used for evaluation and trial installation work; the tenth and eleventh P–82Bs were converted into the prototype P–82C and P–82D night fighters. The fourth B model was fitted with retractable pylons under the outer wings that could carry a total of ten HVAR rocket projectiles in two tiers of five each side, but these pylons could not take bombs or drop tanks, and so the cluster-type installation previously mentioned was used for rocket projectiles. The eight-gun pod developed for the B model was likewise not adopted for operational use, but a rather similar pod housing a forward oblique camera, a tri-metrogon photo unit and three vertical cameras was developed at Eglin Air Force base in 1948 and fitted to the thirteenth P–82B, which was then flown by the Photo Test Squadron of the 3200th Proof Test Group. This variant was known unofficially at Eglin as the RF–82B, the P–82 having become the F–82 under the new designation system of June 1948, and although extensively evaluated at Eglin, the Twin Mustang was not adopted for the photo reconnaissance role. The RF–82B variant, like the other B models, could carry four 310 US gal drop tanks under the outer wings, which gave it the exceptional estimated range of nearly 4,000 miles—longer than that of many airliners.

A practical demonstration of this range was given on 28 February 1947 with the ninth P–82B, 44–65168 named 'Betty Jo' after the wife of the pilot, Lt Colonel Robert E. Thacker, who with Lt J. M. Ard as co-pilot, flew it non-stop over a distance of 4,968 miles from Hickam Field, Hawaii, to La Guardia Airport, New York. An extra fuel tank was also installed in each fuselage just aft of the pilots' seats, and the guns and armour were removed; the total fuel load was 2,215 US gal, and 'Betty Jo' took off at a gross weight of about 30,000lb. The flight was completed in 14 hours, 31 minutes, 50 seconds at an average speed of

342mph, which was slower than predicted because failure of the electric release gear prevented three of the four drop tanks being jettisoned, the one that did go falling into the sea about 100 miles west of San Francisco. And because an autopilot was not fitted, the two pilots had to share the flying of the aircraft over a fourteen-hour spell. A Twin Mustang was entered in the speed section of the international air race from London to Christchurch in New Zealand which started from London Heathrow on 8 October 1953 but, like most of the other interesting entries for this race, it was withdrawn and in the end only five Canberra bombers made up the speed section of this contest. A P–82 was also used to test fly the 20in diameter Marquardt ramjet engine that had previously flown in a P–51D, and the P–82 was also provided on loan to the us Navy by the USAF to test a pilot ejector seat; following these trials the Navy expressed its satisfaction with the British Martin-Baker ejector seat, and later ordered Martin-Baker seats for several of its jets.

The tenth and eleventh P–82Bs, 44–65169 and 44–65170, were converted respectively into the P–82C and P–82D prototype night fighters, both these versions featuring radar (both the scanner dish and the transmitting/receiving equipment) installed in a large radar pod mounted under the centre section; the length of the pod was dictated by the need to place the radar scanner ahead of the airscrew discs. The P–82C had SCR–720 radar, like the Northrop P–61 Black Widow for which the Twin Mustang was being put forward as a replacement, whereas the D model had the newer AN/APS–4 radar in the centre pod. Both versions had the radar display and controls in the starboard cockpit, and armament and external 'stores' were the same as the P–82B. The Twin Mustang's potentialities as a night fighter were good enough for it to be one of the few piston-engined combat

The ninth P–82B, 44–65168 'Betty Jo', on 28
February 1947 was flown non-stop from Hickam
Field, Hawaii, to New York's La Guardia airport
by Lt Col R. E. Thacker and Lt J. M. Ard;
this P–82B was named after the colonel's wife and
the photo here was taken before the record flight
with the name misspelt as 'Betty Joe', the final
'e' being deleted before the flight was made
(*RIC*)

The first P–82B, 44–65160: PQ–160, was later used to flight-test the 20in diameter Marquardt ramjet engine, mounted under the centre section, that had also been test-flown in a P–51D and was intended for the Martin Gorgon IV air-to-surface winged missile (*RIC*)

This view of an F–82E night fighter emphasizes the length of the centre-section radar pod (*RIC*)

aircraft in the first post-war defence budget of fiscal year 1946. Two production versions of the C and D models, 100 F–82Fs and 50 F–82Gs, were ordered in September and October 1946, although nine F models and five Gs were completed as F–82H cold-weather variants for service in Alaska.

But first there was the P–82E, a long-range escort fighter of which 100 had been ordered on 12 December 1945; this reverted to the Allison V–1710 engine for the first time in a production version of the Mustang since the P–51A and A–36A. Two 1,600hp (maximum take-off) V–1710–143 and 145 engines drove 'handed' Aeroproducts four-bladed airscrews which, unlike (of course) those of the single-engined Mustangs, were fully feathering; with water injection, these powerplants developed 1,930hp at sea level and 1,700hp at 21,000ft, and had two-stage

The F–82E long-range escort fighter, of which 100 were ordered, had Allison V–1710–143 and 145 engines; this is the second E model. One F–82E was fitted for test purposes with four Ryan XAAM-A-1 air-to-air missiles under the outer wings (*RIC*)

superchargers. The E model had an auto-pilot and the same armament as the P–82B, and could carry the same external 'stores', including the eight-gun pod which, like the six centre-section machine-guns, carried 400 rounds per gun. Only two of the outer wing pylons had fuel lines enabling them to carry the 310 gal drop tanks, and with these two tanks and 576gal of internal fuel the total fuel capacity was 1,196 us gal. With two drop tanks the combat radius was 1,123 miles cruising at an average of 300mph at 25,000ft, the endurance being eight hours. F–82E deliveries began early in 1948, the E model going exclusively to the 27th Fighter Group at McChord Field, Washington, which comprised the 522nd, 523rd and 524th Fighter Squadrons. The 27th was assigned to the newly formed Strategic Air Command and, with the Cold War intensifying, much of the Group's training was based on possible escort missions for B–29 and B–50 Superfortresses to targets in the Soviet Union. After just over two years' service with the 27th, the F–82E was replaced by the F–84E Thunderjets with

First production version of the Twin Mustang was the P–82B, of which only 20 were completed out of 500 ordered; seen here is P–82B–1–NA 44–65173: FQ–173 with 'stores' pylons under the outer wings (*CWC*)

which the group re-equipped.

As previously mentioned fourteen of the F and G models were completed as the cold weather F–82H, these being 'winterised' for operations from Alaska bases, with modified systems and improved heating, but otherwise equivalent operationally to the F–82G. The F and G models both had the same radar pod as the P–82C and D, the G having SCR–720C radar (as did the F–82H) and the F having an AN/APG–28 set. A comprehensive range of equipment for all-weather flying, such as a glide-path receiver and marker beacon, was carried, and AN/APS–13 tail-warning radar was fitted, this scanning about 4,000ft to the rear of the aircraft and activating a door-bell type alarm very loudly just behind the pilot if a potential enemy aircraft came up from behind; a red light would also come on just above the gunsight. The added weight of specialist night fighter equipment restricted the underwing bomb load to a still very respectable 2,000lb and, like the F–82E, the F and G models could also carry twenty rocket projectiles under the outer wings in four clusters of five, or two 310gal drop tanks.

Korean service

Deliveries of the F–82F and F–82G night fighters were made during 1948 and early 1949, these versions re-equipping a number of units still flying Northrop P–61 Black Widows. The F models went to the 325th Fighter (All-Weather) Group, which comprised the 317th, 318th and 319th Squadrons, the 51st Fighter (Intercepter) Group,

which consisted of the 16th, 25th and 26th Fighter Interception Squadrons, and the 52nd Fighter (All-Weather) Group, comprising the 2nd and 5th Fighter All-Weather Squadrons. The F–82Gs went to the 347th Fighter (All-Weather) Group, consisting of the 4th, 68th and 339th Fighter (All-Weather) Squadrons, and on the outbreak of the Korean War on 25 June 1950 the 347th's Twin Mustangs were the only fighters in the Far East Air Force with sufficient range to fly sorties over Korea from their base at Itazuke in southern Japan. From there they flew patrols from local Korean bases such as Suwon (K–13), attacked targets of opportunity and flew close support and ground attack missions in support of United Nations forces, sometimes using napalm. It was while covering the evacuation of Americans from Suwon that an F–82G of the 68th Squadron, one of eleven on patrol, scored the USAF's first air-to-air victory of the Korean War when it shot down a Yak that had tried to shoot down the No 4 man in the formation; all eleven F–82Gs went after it and there is some doubt as to who actually made the kill, the official USAF history crediting 1st Lt William G. 'Skeeter' Hudson, although it may well have been the No 4 man, 1st Lt 'Chalky' Moran, and both Moran and Hudson were credited with a kill in this engagement, the former with a Yak–9

fighter and the latter with a Yak–11 trainer. A Lavochkin La–7 fighter was also credited to Major J. Little, leading a flight of the 339th Squadron in this encounter.

The F–82H was also in action from the very start of the Korean War, equipping the 449th Fighter (All-Weather) Squadron, an Air Defence Command unit at Ladd Air Force Base near Anchorage. From here four F–82Hs were detached to Marks Air Force Base, Nome, to fly patrols over the Bering Straits region covering the Diomede Islands, St Lawrence and Sledge Islands. The F–82Hs also took photographs of a number of sites on the Soviet mainland, the radar operators using hand-held cameras; it was not thought advisable to risk sending Strategic Air Command's Convair RB–36 or Boeing RB–47 Stratojets to do this job, presumably because of the consequences that could flow from an American bomber's being brought down in this area at such a time of tension. The loss of a fighter, even an all-weather F–82H, on the Soviet side of the Bering Straits, could be more easily explained away as navigational error or by the atrocious weather conditions of this region. The F–82Hs obtained photos of a number of locations on the Soviet side, principally around the edge of the Chukotski Peninsula, flying in pairs for safety although initially, for a few weeks, no Russian fighters were to be seen; about the end of July 1950, a few

Lavochkin La–9s and La–11s began to appear. The Russians would usually try and get between the F–82s and their base at Nome, but the Twin Mustangs' speed enabled them to escape and there were no successful Russian interceptions; these sorties ended after a short time. The 449th Squadron began to re-equip with Lockheed F–94 Starfire jets before the end of 1950, although a few F–82s remained in use for two more years to give close support to Army combat units in Alaska. The last two F–82s were grounded at the end of 1953, marking the end of the type's operational career with the USAF, by whom it had been the last piston-engined fighter to be ordered in quantity, and the last such to be operational with the USAF. The last Twin Mustang to be built, an F–82G, was delivered in April 1949. The Twin Mustang was well liked by its pilots and carried on its single-engined predecessor's tradition of outstanding performance, being made obsolete by the jets. The sole surviving F–82 flying, registered N12102 (ex–F–82B 44–65162), was restored to airworthiness in 1977 by the Confederate Air Force at Harlingen, Texas.

American flair and British quality
Born of a British requirement, the Mustang combined in a unique degree the American flair and enthusiasm for new technology ideas such as the laminar flow wing with British engineering quality and mechanical excellence in the shape of the Rolls-Royce Merlin to produce what was arguably the most outstanding single-seater piston-

121

engined fighter of the war. Designed to a seemingly impossible time-scale by a firm with no previous experience of such a high-performance aircraft, it might so easily have been at best a partial success, at worst a failure—just another interesting prototype for the footnotes of aviation history. Yet its design was inspired, and a wonderful example of what can happen when a talented design team is given its head without being tied down to a detailed official specification. The Mustang is unique, furthermore, among its contemporaries in being modified for racing to an even greater extent, perhaps, than it has been for war; that it continues to be modified by racing pilots, those exacting judges of aeronautical form, nearly forty years after it first flew is perhaps the finest tribute of all to this classic design.

Leading members of the Mustang design team: (*left to right*) Larry Waite, Raymond H. Rice, vice-president in charge of engineering, and Edgar Schmued, chief designer

Appendix

MUSTANG SPECIFICATIONS
Dimensions: Span, 37ft 0$\frac{5}{16}$in (11·27m); length (P–51D), 32ft 3$\frac{1}{4}$in (9·75m); height, 13ft 8in (4·16m); wing area (gross), 233·19sq ft (21·66sq m); dihedral, 5°; undercarriage track, 11ft 10in (3·86m).
Dimensions (**F–82G Twin Mustang**): Span, 51ft 7in (15·73m); length, 42ft 2$\frac{1}{2}$in (12·86m); height, 13ft 9$\frac{1}{2}$in (4·21m); wing area, 417·6sq ft (38·79sq m); aspect ratio, 6·28; dihedral, 6° on outer wings; undercarriage track, 16ft 8$\frac{1}{2}$in (5·09m).

Weights	**P–51A**	**P–51B**	**P–51D**
Empty			7,125lb (3,230kg)
Combat			10,100lb (4,581kg)
Gross	9,000lb (4,083kg)		11,100lb (5,035kg)
Max loaded	10,600lb (4,808kg) with two 150 US gal drop tanks	11,200lb (5,080kg) with two 1,000lb bombs	11,600lb (5,261kg) with two 108 US gal drop tanks

Weights	**Cavalier 2000, 2500**	**Turbo Mustang 3**	**F–82G Twin Mustang**
Empty	7,500lb (3,402kg)	6,816lb (3,092kg)	15,997lb (7,254kg)
Max payload	3,000lb (1,361kg)		
Combat			21,810lb (9,902kg)
Max landing weight	9,200lb (4,174kg)		
Max loaded	10,500lb (4,763kg)	14,000lb (6,350kg)	
Max take-off and landing			25,891lb (11,755kg) with 20 HVARS

Performance	**Mustang I**	**P–51B**	**P–51D**
Max speed	390mph at 8,000ft (628km/h at 2,439m)	437mph at 30,000ft (703km/h at 9,145m)	437mph at 25,000ft (703km/h at 7,620m)
Initial rate of climb	8·1 minutes to 15,000ft (4,572m)	3,900ft/min (1,189m/min)	3,475ft/min (1,060m/min)
Service ceiling	32,000ft (9,755m)	42,500ft (12,952m)	41,900ft (12,770m)
Max range	Up to 1,000 miles (1,609km)	1,710 miles (2,751km)	2,080 miles (3,231km) (absolute) with two 100 US gal drop tanks
Normal range		1,300 miles (2,090km)	

Performance	**Cavalier**	**Turbo Mustang 3**	**F–82G Twin Mustang***
Max speed	457mph at 28,000ft (735km/h at 8,535m)		460mph at 21,000ft (740km/h at 6,400m)
Max cruising speed	424mph at 30,000ft (682km/h at 9,145m)	540mph (869km/h)	288mph at 25,000ft (average) (463km/h at 7,620m)
Initial rate of climb	2,550ft/min (777m/min)		950ft/min (290m/min)
Service ceiling	42,000ft (12,800m)		28,300ft (8,626m)
Max range	2,500 miles (4,020km) (Cavalier 2500)	2,300 miles (3,700km) (ferrying range)	
Normal range			2,240 miles (3,604km) (combat range)

*As for night fighter mission with two drop tanks

Bibliography

In addition to such sources as personal notes and newspaper cuttings, the following are the principal books and periodicals drawn upon for information on the North American Mustang:

Birch, David. 'Those Mustang Xs', *Air Britain Digest* (August 1970)

Brickhill, Paul. *The Dam Busters* (Evans Bros, 1951)

Carson, L. K. 'The Making of the Mustang', *Wings* (June 1976)

Destiny Can Wait: The History of the Polish Air Force in Great Britain (various authors) (Heinemann, 1950)

Freeman, Roger A. *Mustang at War* (Ian Allan, 1976)

Green, William. *Famous Fighters of the Second World War* (Macdonald & Jane's, 1957)

Green, W., Swanborough, G., Thompson, W. 'F-82: Killers over Korea', *Air Enthusiast Six* (March–June 1978)

Jane's All the World's Aircraft (Macdonald & Jane's)

Kinnert, Reed. *Racing Planes and Air Races* (Vol IV and subsequent volumes) (Aero Publishers)

Swanborough, Gordon. *North American Album* (Ian Allan, 1973)

The Aeroplane Spotter
Air-Britain publications
Air Pictorial
Flight International
Flying Review International

Acknowledgements

The author is particularly indebted to Gene Boswell, Public Relations Photo Services, Rockwell International Corporation (which was created by the merger of North American Rockwell and Rockwell Manufacturing in February 1973), to Harry Holmes, Howard Levy and Arthur Pearcy for their assistance in providing photographs for this book, and to Clifford Minney, who prepared the line drawings.

Acknowledgement is also made to the following sources for photos, abbreviated in the captions as indicated in brackets:
Air Pictorial (Air Pic)
N. L. Avery (*NLA*)
Cavalier Aircraft Corporation (*CAV*)
via Charles W. Cain archives (*CWC*)
Flightlines International (*FL*)
J. M. G. Gradidge (*JMGG*)
H. Holmes (*HH*)
Imperial War Museum (*IWM*)
Howard Levy (*HL*)
Arthur Pearcy (*AP*)
Bruce Robertson (*BR*)
Rockwell International Corp (*RIC*)
Rolls-Royce (*RR*)
US Official (*USO*)

Index